Cases in
Corporate Governance

Cases in
Corporate Governance

ROBERT WEARING

SAGE Publications
London ● Thousand Oaks ● New Delhi

Learning Resources
Centre

13012622

First published 2005

 SAGE Publications
1 Oliver's Yard
55 City Road
London EC1Y 1SP

SAGE Publications Inc
2455 Teller Road
Thousand Oaks, California 91320

SAGE Publications India Pvt Ltd
B-42, Panchsheel Enclave
Post Box 4109
New Delhi 110 017

Library of Congress Control Number: 2005901202

A catalogue record for this book is available from
the British Library

ISBN 1-4129-0876-0
ISBN 1-4129-0877-9 (pbk)

Typeset by M Rules
Printed and bound in Great Britain by Athenaeum Press, Gateshead

Contents

List of illustrations

FIGURES

TABLES

Preface

Corporate governance is a fascinating subject which encompasses a number of diverse areas of study including management, finance and accounting as well as having implications for legal and political processes. This book intends to provide insights into current issues in corporate governance by examining the links between corporate governance theory, regulation and practice. The case studies contained in the book examine the circumstances of companies where corporate governance is seen to be an issue.

An important feature of the book is the nine selected cases, some of which have been important in influencing codes and regulations of corporate behaviour in both the UK and the USA. The cases are designed to reinforce the reader's understanding of the conditions under which corporate governance can break down and what is involved in trying to define 'good' corporate governance.

In corporate governance there are not always 'right' and 'wrong' answers. Because of the nature of the topic there is never likely to be complete consensus on which system of governance is ideal under all possible circumstances and this aspect makes it an intriguing area for study. It is hoped that *Cases in Corporate Governance* will stimulate interest in the subject and encourage discussion of the various issues identified in the case studies.

Robert T. Wearing
University of Essex

Acknowledgements

I would like to express my appreciation to Delia Martinez Alfonso at SAGE Publications for her encouragement for writing the book. I would also like to thank Carmen A. Li of Essex University for helpful comments and suggestions on the typescript, although of course I accept full responsibility for any remaining errors.

Glossary

ACCA	Association of Chartered Certified Accountants
ASB	Accounting Standards Board
AT&T	American Telephone and Telegraph
BCCI	Bank of Credit and Commerce International
BPC	British Printing Corporation
BPCC	British Printing and Communications Corporation
BT	British Telecom
CALPERS	California Public Employees' Retirement System
CEO	Chief Executive Officer
CFO	Chief Financial Officer
CONSOB	Commissione Nazionale per le Società e la Borsa [Italian state regulator]
DTI	Department of Trade and Industry
EES	Enron Energy Services
FASB	Financial Accounting Standards Board
FSA	Financial Services Authority
FTSE	Financial Times Stock Exchange
GAAP	Generally Accepted Accounting Principles
ICAEW	Institute of Chartered Accountants in England and Wales
IEA	International Energy Agency
LDDS	Long Distance Discount Services
MBA	Master in Business Administration
MCC	Maxwell Communications Corporation
MGN	Mirror Group Newspapers
MP	Member of Parliament
MTM	Mark-to-market
NASDAQ	National Association of Securities Dealers Automated Quotation
NYSE	New York Stock Exchange
OFR	Operating and Financial Review
OTC	Over The Counter
PCAOB	Public Company Accounting Oversight Board
PwC	PricewaterhouseCoopers
RRR	Reserve Replacement Ratio

SEC	Securities and Exchange Commission
SFA	Securities and Futures Authority
SFO	Serious Fraud Office
SIMEX	Singapore International Monetary Exchange
SPE	Special Purpose Entity
SPV	Special Purpose Vehicle
SSAP	Statement of Standard Accounting Practice
TML	Transmanche-Link [Eurotunnel contractor]
TMT	Technology, Media and Telecommunications

Introduction

The focus of this book is on case studies of companies that have experienced problems with their corporate governance procedures. Nine case studies are presented here and it is hoped that the reader will find the material both interesting and instructive. Some common themes tend to run through these cases, such as charismatic and powerful business leaders, companies experiencing rapid and unsustainable rates of growth, unreasonably optimistic market expectations of future growth and unnecessarily complicated organization. Not all the companies discussed in this book have collapsed. Shell, for example (see Chapter 12), operates profitably but its corporate governance procedures have been the subject of debate in the media because of its overstatement of oil and gas reserves, announced in January 2004.

Many believe that robust systems of corporate governance are important for both large and small organizations. The purpose of this book is to provide some insight into why corporate governance can break down and, by discussing case studies, to look at what might be done to remedy such situations. In addition, two chapters provide an introduction to corporate governance theory and corporate governance regulation.[1]

This book can be thought of as a supplementary source of material, which encourages topical discussion in seminars and classes. Each case study in the book is designed to introduce the reader to a factual 'real life' episode which has corporate governance implications. Each case is designed to reinforce the reader's knowledge and understanding of corporate governance theory and help to explain why corporate governance codes and regulations are widely thought to be essential in modern business life. It is intended that each case will motivate students to discuss, in a seminar or class setting, the reasons why corporate governance failed, or was seen to be inadequate.

This book does not pretend to offer easy solutions to the problems identified in the case studies. However, certain elements and themes can be identified, such as the problems that can occur when the chairman or chief executive becomes too powerful (or indeed is the same person) or when the non-executive directors are seen to be lacking in independence and authority. The reader is encouraged to adopt an independent and analytical approach to the case material and use the discussion section to reinforce their understanding of corporate governance issues.

Corporate governance cases and their ramifications tend to be in the public eye over a long period of time. When court action is involved, cases can take many years to resolve. Cases such as BCCI and Polly Peck came to the public's attention in the early 1990s, but legal disputes are still ongoing.

Case studies have a valuable role to play in affording a deeper understanding of corporate governance issues. Case-study analysis can also assist social scientists in the development of theories and hypotheses, which can then be subject to more rigorous scientific investigation. At the same time, it is important to be aware of the difficulties involved in trying to derive general conclusions from a case study.[2]

The book is structured as follows: the two chapters on the theory and regulation of corporate governance are followed by nine case studies, with a final chapter which offers a synthesis of conclusions.

Chapter 2 on corporate governance theory reviews the development of the modern corporation and discusses principal–agent theory and stakeholder theory as suitable frameworks for analysing corporate governance problems.

Chapter 3 on corporate governance regulation discusses the development of *The Combined Code on Corporate Governance* in the UK and Sarbanes–Oxley legislation in the USA. It is debatable whether these codes and regulations can ever be sufficient on their own to tackle 'weak' corporate governance, and there have been suggestions that a change in business culture is required. Also, when framing corporate governance codes and regulations, a suitable balance needs to be struck between the demands of managers and the needs of stakeholders. Finally, the chapter closes by suggesting that some answers to the question 'What is good corporate governance?' may be found by analysing and dissecting cases where many observers would agree that a definite failure in corporate governance procedures has occurred.

Chapter 4 discusses the case of the Robert Maxwell's business empire. In November 1991 Robert Maxwell, an apparently successful business leader with important newspaper and publishing interests, disappeared at sea from his yacht *Lady Ghislaine* and it soon became apparent that his business empire was in serious financial difficulties. Employees who lost substantial pension entitlements were particularly disadvantaged. Chapter 5 discusses issues arising from the collapse of Polly Peck, a large UK quoted company, in October 1990. In 2004 this case had not yet been fully resolved, mainly because the former chairman and chief executive is effectively in exile in northern Cyprus.

Chapter 6 discusses the case of the Bank of Credit and Commerce International (BCCI), which was forced by regulators to suspend its operations in July 1991. The Bank of England's regulatory practices were subsequently criticized in an official report the following year.

Chapter 7 addresses the financial scandal surrounding Enron, one of the world's largest energy groups, operating in the USA. The company filed for bankruptcy in 2001 and it was discovered that reported profits had been substantially overstated. Chapter 8 discusses another corporate failure, WorldCom, which became bankrupt in July 2002. A main concern was that capital expenditures were found to have been misclassified. It is widely believed that Enron and WorldCom were crucial factors in getting the Sarbanes–Oxley legislation onto the statute books.

Chapter 9 discusses the events surrounding the financial collapse of Parmalat, an Italian multinational company. In 2004 senior executives of the company were facing charges of false accounting in connection with the collapse.

Chapter 10 examines the relationship between the company and shareholders of Eurotunnel. Eurotunnel came to the market in 1987, but its actual capital expenditures proved to be much higher than those projected in the original prospectus. In addition, projected revenues proved to be substantially overstated. This case specifically addresses the issue of how shareholders (as principals) can effectively monitor the actions of managers (as agents). Chapter 11 discusses the case of Barings Bank which collapsed in 1995 following unauthorized trading by one of its derivatives traders, Nick Leeson.

Chapter 12 examines events at Shell. In January 2004 Shell announced that it had overstated its oil and gas reserves, and this case study examines the subsequent impact on the share price and how the company has attempted to reform its organization structures and corporate governance practices.

Chapter 13 attempts to draw together the arguments and issues raised in the previous chapters and offers suggestions and recommendations for improving corporate governance. This chapter aims to show that the study of real-world examples of corporate governance is necessarily 'backward looking', but it is through this type of analysis that lessons can be learned for the future and relevant theories and hypotheses can be developed.

Finally, it should be noted that the discussion questions, which appear at the end of each case study, have not been formulated with the intention of leading to a 'right' answer since there is unlikely to be complete consensus on what is 'good' corporate governance. Managers of companies are more likely to be aware of the costs of corporate governance, in terms of resources devoted to compliance with codes and regulations. On the other hand, stakeholders are more likely to be aware of the benefits, which could prevent or avoid loss of shareholders' capital, loss of employment, loss of pension entitlements and loss of amounts owing from failed companies.

REFERENCES

Mallin, C.A. (2004) *Corporate Governance*. Oxford: Oxford University Press.
Monks, R.A.G. and Minow, N. (2004) *Corporate Governance,* 3rd edn. Oxford: Blackwell.
Ryan, B., Scapens, R.W. and Theobald, M. (1992) *Research Method and Methodology in Finance and Accounting*. London: Academic Press.
Solomon, J. and Solomon, A. (2004) *Corporate Governance and Accountability*. Chichester: Wiley.

NOTES

1 For a fuller discussion of the theory, regulation and practice of corporate governance, texts such as Mallin (2004), Monks and Minow (2004), or Solomon and Solomon (2004) are recommended.

2 See, for instance, chapter 7 of Ryan, Scapens and Theobald (1992) for a discussion of the advantages and disadvantages of case-study research.

Corporate Governance Theory

Since the nineteenth century, when incorporation was first introduced into the UK, there have been significant changes to the way firms are organized and financed. In order to appreciate how theorists have tried to make sense of corporate governance issues, we can refer to two widely discussed 'theories' or approaches commonly used to attempt to understand how corporations are governed and how the system of corporate governance can be improved. The first approach is often called principal–agent theory (or agency theory). The second approach is referred to as stakeholder theory.

In the literature on the theory of the firm, we soon encounter the term 'separation of ownership and control'. What does this mean? If we go back to the nineteenth century, many of the largest companies were both owned *and* controlled by their founding proprietors. Over time the original founders were able to accumulate substantial wealth as profits were reinvested in their enterprises. But, despite this, the proprietors began to realize that their own resources were not sufficient to finance sustained growth. Often they were in a position to raise additional loan capital, which would not dilute their own shareholding and therefore not affect control of the company.

But there is a limit to how much debt finance a company can sensibly carry. And, in order to maintain their competitive advantage and benefit from economies of scale, there was an inexorable need to grow in size. Therefore they needed to raise additional share capital via the stock markets. This meant that their personal shareholding became smaller relative to the company as a whole. In addition, as they retired or died, their shares were parcelled out amongst their descendants. In the early part of the twentieth century it became evident that the largest shareholdings were becoming fragmented and dispersed. In other words there was a reduction in ownership concentration.

OWNERSHIP

What do we mean by ownership? It is a truism to say that the shareholders own the company. Unfortunately this statement offers us little insight into complex corporate governance relationships; indeed, as well pointed out by Blair (1995), it often obscures the important issues instead of illuminating them. One explanation of the distinctive features of share ownership compares it with ownership of a physical object, such as a house:

> When I tell you that I own my house, you will infer that I decide who may enter it or live in it, and who not; that I determine how it will be furnished and decorated; and that I have the right to dispose of all or part of it and keep the proceeds for my own benefit. When I buy a share in BT [British Telecom] I enjoy none of these rights in relation to BT, except a limited version of the last. (Kay and Silberston, 1995: 87)

This is really the essence of the problem. Particularly in the case of small shareholders, the owner's rights are very limited and in practice amount to receiving dividends and disposing of the shares, usually because the company has performed poorly in the past and is unlikely to do better in the future, or because the company has performed well in the past but is unlikely to do as well in the future. So this is a relatively passive form of ownership. It is true that a shareholder has a right to vote in the annual general meeting (AGM) on critical matters such as the election of directors. But in reality, and given that a large company can have hundreds of millions of ordinary shares, the chances of a small shareholder swaying the balance in an AGM are about as likely as a single voter determining the choice of government in a general election.

In fact the issue of ownership is even more complex than the above analogy suggests. In reality, even though I own a house or motor car, I cannot do whatever I like with it, since I am subject to other constraints – such as building regulations in the case of housing and safety legislation in the case of motor cars. And in the case of share ownership, there are subtle distinctions in the difference between influence and control depending, not only on the absolute proportion of shares held in a company, but also the absolute proportion relative to blocks of shareholdings owned by others. For example, if I hold 10 per cent of the shares in a company and the remainder are highly fragmented, it is quite possible that I could exert some influence on the board of directors. But if the remaining shares include two blocks of 30 per cent each (and the owners are in collusion), then my 10 per cent might give me very little influence indeed.

In the nineteenth century it could be reasonably argued in many cases that the owners were in control, that in fact the owners were also the managers. As we move into the twentieth century, the managers, a distinct and separate professional elite, are said to be in control. Berle and Means (1932) proposed the separation of ownership and control as an important explanation for corporate behaviour and the problems confronting owners (fragmented and dispersed shareholders) who attempt to exert their rights over the managers who have gained control in the 'modern' corporation.

They recognized that control can rarely be sharply segregated or defined. They did, however, distinguish the following five major types of control:

1 Control through almost complete ownership
2 Majority control
3 Control through a legal device without majority ownership
4 Minority control
5 Management control

Although Berle and Means (1932) recognized that in some cases a firm could be dictated to by an outside party, for instance if it were heavily in debt to a bank, they concluded that in most cases 'the control' resided in the group of individuals who have the power to select the directors.

PRINCIPAL–AGENT THEORY

The development of agency theory is often traced back to Berle and Means (1932), although some writers suggest that one can go back to Adam Smith in 1776 and his influential book *The Wealth of Nations*. Letza, Sun and Kirkbride (2004) point out that the agency problem was effectively identified by Adam Smith when he argued that company directors were not likely to be as careful with other people's money as with their own.

Subsequently the firm was viewed as the nexus of a set of contracting relationships among individuals. Most important among these was the agency relationship, which has been defined as 'a contract under which one or more persons (the principal(s)) engage another person (the agent) to perform some service on their behalf which involves delegating some decision making authority to the agent' (Jensen and Meckling, 1976: 308). The agency relationship can be a problem because the agent may not always act in the best interests of the principal(s). Agency costs are then incurred, which include monitoring costs incurred by the principal, bonding costs incurred by the agent, and reductions in welfare resulting from decisions taken by the agent which are not consistent with maximisation of the principal's welfare. Moreover, Jensen and Meckling were aware that it was costly, if not impossible, to write contracts which would clearly delineate the rights of principals for all possible contingencies.

Shleifer and Vishny (1997) argue that the agency problem is an important element of the contractual view of the firm. The analysis then focuses on the impossibility of writing complete contracts, and the complexities arising from incomplete contracts. Hart (1995) offers three reasons why principals and agents tend to write incomplete contracts. Firstly, it is difficult for people to think ahead and plan for all possible contingencies; secondly, it is hard for the contracting parties to negotiate effectively, especially where prior experience may not be a helpful guide; thirdly, it is difficult for plans to be written down in such a way that an outside authority, such as a court, will be able to interpret and enforce the contract.

Moreover Aghion and Bolton (1992) argue that – as a result of contractual incompleteness and wealth constraints – it is not possible to resolve all potential conflicts between the agent and the principal.

In a traditional shareholding perspective, the corporation can be viewed as a 'legal instrument for shareholders to maximize their own interests – investment returns' (Letza, Sun and Kirkbride, 2004: 243). Within this model, it is often assumed that the managers are more/better informed about the firm than are the shareholders. In other words there is information asymmetry: agents have better access to information than shareholders. In an agency setting, principals can attempt to overcome the information asymmetry by monitoring management, but this is a costly activity for individual principals. The overall costs of information-gathering can be reduced if systems are put into place to provide relevant information to all shareholders. For example, this could be the provision of regular, audited financial reports or ensuring that systems operate to deter agents from benefiting from the use of their privileged knowledge (for instance, by using inside information to indulge in share dealing).

Market for corporate control

Supporters of agency theory regard the market for corporate control as an important way to discipline the agents (the managers) and motivate them to act in the best interests of the principals (the shareholders). The mechanism for this is the desire of managers to avoid a hostile takeover of their company (since they would most probably lose their jobs). To this end, the managers try to maintain a 'high' share valuation. High share values have a number of benefits for managers. For one thing, a high share value means that it is less expensive to obtain extra finance from the stock market. But the main benefit to managers – in respect of their own job security – is that a high share valuation makes it more expensive for a predator to gain control. In an agency setting, where managers feel that they need to satisfy the needs of shareholders alone, then a high share valuation is also likely to be attractive to the principals.

It is of course important that, in achieving a high share valuation, the managers do not focus on short-term objectives, since such a policy could be inconsistent with achieving a high share valuation in the longer term. Companies which adhere to short-term objectives might focus too intensely on particular financial indicators, such as short-term profit or earnings per share. It is also important that the financial reporting system is sufficiently robust to ensure that markets are not 'fooled' by the manipulation of profit-and-loss account data by the agents. The perceived problem is that management incentives may be set in such a way that they focus too much on short-term objectives. This is seen as being harmful to a company's long-term prospects because, for instance, over-emphasizing short-term profitability might mean that insufficient research and development are carried out. These types of expenditure tend to have pay-offs in the future, pay-offs which may be uncertain – but, for many companies, investment in research and development is essential for long-term survival.

In recent times, British and American companies have devoted considerable attention to shareholder interests and there are plenty of observers who would agree with this focus. Why should this be the case? Kay and Silberston (1995) argue that this situation arises because of the threat of hostile takeover. In other words, a main threat to the directors remaining in office is if another company is prepared to offer a sufficiently attractive amount to buy out the existing shareholders. A hostile predator would only be able to do this if the target company share price were below the average for similar firms in the same industry. If a company is not efficient in the way it uses its assets, a predator can gain control and then make more productive use of the assets; as a result, profits should increase and share prices rise, to reflect the anticipated increase in future profits. In order to counter this possibility, the existing management must carry out policies that maintain a 'high' share price, thereby making it more expensive for a potential predator to try to gain control.

STAKEHOLDER THEORY

Some argue that the principal–agent model appears to focus exclusively on the interests of shareholders. But it may happen that managers are over-concerned with shareholders who are interested only in short-term profits and consequently managers neglect the long term. Blair (1995) refers to this situation as 'market myopia'. Short-run gains are made at the expense of long-term performance. One solution to this problem would be to encourage longer-term shareholding. But a more fundamental concern is that 'what is optimal for shareholders often is not optimal for the rest of society. That is, the corporate policies that generate the most wealth for shareholders may not be the policies that generate the greatest total social wealth' (Blair, 1995: 13).

This leads us on to a consideration of stakeholder theory, which stands in direct contrast to principal–agent theory. Whereas principal–agent theory has an underlying assumption that profit maximization is the main motivation for a company's strategy and tactics, stakeholder theory instead stresses the importance of all parties who are affected, either directly or indirectly, by a firm's operations. Stakeholder refers to any party that has a 'stake' in the company; while this obviously includes the shareholders and directors (principal and agent in agency theory), other parties such as employees, government, customers, suppliers, bankers and the like can also be stakeholders. Indeed, the list can be extended to include the general public, if it is accepted that a firm can affect the public through its actions on the environment.

> Boards must understand that they are the representatives of all the important stakeholders in the firm – all those whose investments in physical or human capital are at risk. Thus, individuals who explicitly represent critical stakeholders should be put on boards, to give those stakeholders some assurance that their interests will be taken into account. (Blair, 1995: 326)

Although conflicts of interest can result, these conflicts may be reduced by ensuring that all stakeholders receive an equity stake proportional to their firm-specific investments.

The conventional wisdom is that shareholders receive dividends and capital gains as a reward for risking their investment in a company (although modern finance theory shows that firm-specific risk can be reduced through portfolio diversification). But stakeholder theory makes the important point that employees also risk their capital, human capital, when they work for a firm. Under stakeholder theory this is just as important an investment as financial capital and one could argue that employees are not in a position to reduce their risk through diversification. Taking suppliers as another stakeholder example, one could argue that a supplier who makes a substantial investment, on a specific product for one customer, is taking a risk that the customer may with little warning turn to another supplier. The equity solution for employee stakeholders suggests itself fairly easily, that is, part-payment in shares in the company. However, the equity solution for other stakeholders, such as a company's supplier or customer, is more problematical.

An interesting example of stakeholder theory being applied in practice is the John Lewis Partnership, which operates department stores in the UK and was founded by John Spedan Lewis in the first half of the twentieth century. One of the principal objectives of the founder was to ensure democracy in the workplace so that the employees could 'share in the advantages of ownership, sharing fairly in the trinity of reward, knowledge and power. In this way, the business would in effect be a partnership and the employees partners in the enterprise' (Graham, 1994: 35). Although a main concern of John Spedan Lewis was for the welfare of the employees, it is clear that his philosophy included providing a service to the general community, that is, effectively extending the scope of the term stakeholder.

It is important to recognize that corporate governance cannot be judged in isolation from the culture in which it operates. Vinten (2001) points out that stakeholder theory is becoming universal, especially outside the Anglo-Saxon world in influential economies such as Japan, France and Germany. In addition, abstract models are criticized on the grounds that they are too far removed from the real-world business environment. Letza, Sun and Kirkbride (2004: 243) argue that such abstract theories 'ignore the continuous change of natural and social realities and distance themselves from the dynamics of corporate governance in practice'. They argue that, with the advent of globalization, 'the boundary of the firm has become blurred in terms of global markets and . . . physical assets are far less important than human resources, knowledge and information'.

Although we might question the relative values attributed to physical assets and human resources, there is little doubt that an increasing concern with and appreciation of human resources is an important factor for supporters of stakeholder theory. Indeed, 'corporate social, ethical and environmental performance are being viewed increasingly by investors as indicators of management and proxies for performance in other areas of business. A company that is well managed is likely to have a good environmental management system and high levels of stakeholder dialogue and engagement' (Solomon and Solomon, 2004: 39).

DISCUSSION

In agency theory, the purpose of the firm is presumed to be the maximization of shareholder value. This is a relatively narrow objective and supporters of stakeholder theory would argue that such a narrow objective is incompatible with the responsibilities of the enlightened modern corporation, which needs to take into account the effect of its actions on working conditions, relations with customers and suppliers, and the environment.

On the other hand, supporters of agency theory would argue that any corporate governance reforms should align managers' interests with shareholder interests, for instance by tying directors' bonuses closely to profitability. The business as a whole would then benefit, since reinvested profits will help to build up the firm's economic resources, thereby allowing for future capital investment and expenditure on worthwhile long-term projects such as research and development. These activities will ultimately benefit other stakeholders. For example, the workforce will benefit from enhanced job security and the environment will benefit through greater investment in more efficient and less harmful industrial processes.

In other words, from an agency perspective, profit maximization is not incompatible with improving the lot of all stakeholders, not just shareholders. In this context a strong, independent element on the board of directors is another way of aligning the interests of principals and agents by allowing the principals to better monitor the actions of agents and thereby (according to Hermalin and Weisbach, 2003) to help solve the principal–agent problem.

Stakeholder theory becomes incompatible with corporate governance when the number of groups identified as stakeholders increases dramatically to the point where the term 'stakeholder' is no longer meaningful for analysis.

Stakeholder theory provides no effective standard against which corporate agents can be judged. Balancing stakeholder interests is an ill-defined notion, which cannot serve as an objective performance measure; managers responsible for interpreting as well as implementing it are effectively left free to pursue their own arbitrary ends. (Sternberg, 1997: 5)

Recently, some features of the agency model and stakeholder theory have been combined in an attempt to make both approaches more appealing.

Gamble and Kelly (2001) argue that incremental changes are taking place that are likely to make the traditional shareholder model more acceptable. These changes are referred to as 'enlightened managerialism' whereby companies have adopted voluntary codes in order to disseminate best practice. In addition, Gamble and Kelly perceive the possibility of an increasingly active shareholder movement. This might be assisted by government modifying the law to ensure that boards of directors are held more accountable to their shareholders. However they acknowledge that increasing share ownership through privatizations has not established a wider share-owning culture. Furthermore, they favour corporate pluralism and a more formal recognition in company governance of the investment and risks incurred by stakeholders (not just shareholders).

The corporate pluralism position on the company in the stakeholding debate proposes to acknowledge the pluralistic structure of the modern company by changing the legal framework to accommodate it. The strength of this perspective is that it offers a way to make the company both more efficient and more legitimate. (Gamble and Kelly, 2001: 115)

Jensen (2001) argues for a modified approach to agency theory and stresses the importance of maximizing firm value: 'two hundred years of work in economics and finance implies that in the absence of externalities and monopoly (and when all goods are priced), social welfare is maximized when each firm in an economy maximizes its total market value' (Jensen, 2001: 297). He acknowledges that a firm cannot maximize its value if it ignores the interest of its stakeholders. Therefore he argues in favour of enlightened value maximization, which he regards as identical to enlightened stakeholder theory. No doubt advocates of stakeholder theory would find it hard to accept the mechanism whereby focusing on firm market-value maximization leads inevitably to social welfare maximization. Nevertheless, leaving this concern to one side, it seems reasonable to accept that multiple objectives mean no objective:

Telling a manager to maximize current profits, market share, future growth in profits, and anything else one pleases will leave that manager with no objective. The result will be confusion and lack of purpose that will fundamentally handicap the firm in its competition for survival. (Jensen, 2001: 301).

Interestingly, Jensen asks why managers and directors of corporations embrace stakeholder theory. Clearly he believes that there are self-interested motives at work:

> Because stakeholder theory provides no definition of 'better', it leaves managers and directors unaccountable for their stewardship of the firm's resources. With no criteria for performance, managers cannot be evaluated in any principled way . . . By expanding the power of managers in this unproductive way, stakeholder theory therefore increases agency costs in the economic system. Viewed in this way it is not surprising that many managers like it. (Jensen, 2001: 305)

This leads Jensen to conclude in favour of enlightened value maximization and enlightened stakeholder theory. In the long run, for a firm to be successful, 'managers must pay attention to all constituencies that can affect the firm' (Jensen, 2001: 304). In other words, for a firm to be successful and survive, it needs to address the needs of all its stakeholders.

Hill and Jones (1992) attempt to modify agency theory in order to analyse stakeholder issues and, in so doing, arrive at a theory of stakeholder-agency. For example, the analysis of issues such as agency costs can be widened to encompass the incentive, monitoring and enforcement structures which involve all stakeholders (not just shareholders) with the agents or managers. In an agency setting, devices set up *ex-ante* (in advance) can help to align the interests of the agents with those of the principals. An example is stock option plans, which are intended to increase agent wealth and shareholder wealth simultaneously. This analysis can be extended to a stakeholder setting and the example usually offered is an *ex-ante* warranty given by management to customers as a means whereby customers can be compensated if the product or service proves to be defective.

When we analyse the principal–agent framework, the focus of attention is essentially on the conflict between the agent and the principal and the problem is to maximize principal wealth and agent wealth while minimizing agency costs. In a stakeholder framework, the problem is somewhat more complex because of the added dimension of conflicts between the various stakeholders. Although the different groups may have competing claims (for example, increased wages would be incompatible with increased dividends, other things being equal), nevertheless 'on a more general level, each group can be seen as having a stake in the continued existence of the firm' (Hill and Jones, 1992: 145) – and this is perhaps the important point: the long-term survival of the firm and therefore the long-term survival of the stakeholders.

Donaldson and Preston (1995) point to the growing debate in the academic and professional management literature over the role of stakeholders, and argue that normative concerns provide a critical underpinning for stakeholder theory. In other words, stakeholder theory is a theory about *what should be*, and not necessarily *what is*. This is an interesting point, since it seems plausible to argue that shareholder theory has evolved out of financial economics, using conventional 'positive' analysis, whereas stakeholder theory is more strongly embedded in a tradition of the moral and philosophical rights of stakeholders. The efficiency argument is perhaps easier to make for shareholder theory than it is for stakeholder theory, but we should not forget that both shareholder theory and stakeholder theory have normative elements.

The concept of limited liability was of major importance in underpinning the growth in early stock markets. The fact that an investor's liability could be limited to the original share subscription and exclude any additional losses made by the firm was a substantial attraction. Monks and Minow (2004) view the notion of limited liability as the benefit an investor receives in return for surrendering direct control of the company's property:

> The shareholder has the exclusive control of the stock itself. But as a condition of the shareholder's limited liability, the shareholder gives up the right to control use of the corporation's property by others. That right is delegated to the management of the corporation. Indeed, it is one of the benefits of the corporate organization to the investor; he can entrust his money to people who have expertise and time that he does not. But it is also one of the drawbacks. Thus it is this separation between ownership and control that has been the focus of the struggles over corporate governance. (Monks and Minow, 2004: 111)

But the entrenched, legal view of a corporation assumes the predominant importance of shareholder interests:

> It has always been permissible, even required, for directors and managers to consider the interests of all stakeholders, as long as they do so in the context of the interests of shareholder value. Courts have upheld a corporation's right to donate corporate funds to charities, for example, if it was in the corporation's long-term interests . . . while it is useful (and cost-effective) for boards to consider the best way to meet the admittedly competing needs of the company's diverse constituencies, it is imperative for them to give shareholders first priority. Only with that as their goal can they serve the other constituencies over the long term. (Monks and Minow, 2004, 51)

Supporters of agency theory point to the market for control and the discipline that it exerts over agents. Although this may be a satisfactory outcome from a shareholder perspective, from a stakeholder perspective the benefits may not always be so obvious. Although being employed in a more profitable firm might have its attractions, there is often the danger that some parts of the target firm (and the associated workforce) could be viewed as redundant. In addition, for those employees who remain in employment in the enlarged corporation, the new management may want to introduce measures that enhance shareholder value, but at the same time act against the interests of the employees. For example, in the UK a number of companies have shifted their employee pension plans from 'defined benefit' schemes to 'defined contribution' schemes. This decision usually benefits shareholders but disadvantages employees.

So far, we have discussed shareholder and stakeholder approaches to corporate governance. But would corporate governance be improved by attempting to modify corporate ethical behaviour? Many large companies issue a business code, sometimes described as a corporate code of ethics or a code of conduct. But we should be aware, as Kaptein (2004) points out, that the existence of a code does not necessarily mean that a company will adhere to it, although its contents will at least indicate what kind of ethics the company claims to uphold. Nevertheless, there are those who believe that corporate governance can be enhanced through wider disclosure of its ethical policies.

It is clear that the relative merits of agency theory and stakeholder theory will be debated for some time to come. Although, for the sake of theoretical analysis, it is useful to identify two distinct approaches to corporate governance – one based on the importance of shareholding and another based on the importance of stakeholding – it is important to remember that, in the real world, governance is likely to lie somewhere between these two extreme positions.

REFERENCES

Aghion, P. and Bolton, P. (1992) 'An incomplete contracts approach to financial contracting', *Review of Economic Studies*, Vol. 59: 473–94.

Berle, A.A. and Means, G.C. (1932) *The Modern Corporation and Private Property*. New York: Macmillan.

Blair, M.M. (1995) *Ownership and control: Rethinking Corporate Governance for the Twenty-First Century*. Washington, DC: The Brookings Institution.

Donaldson, T. and Preston, L.E. (1995) 'The stakeholder theory of the corporation: concepts, evidence and implications', *Academy of Management Review*, Vol. 20, No. 1: 65–91.

Gamble, A. and Kelly, G. (2001) 'Shareholder value and the stakeholder debate in the UK', *Corporate Governance: An International Review*, Vol. 9, No. 2: 110–17.

Graham, P. (1994) 'The registrar in the John Lewis Partnership plc' in G. Vinten (ed) *Whistleblowing: Subversion or corporate citizenship?* London: Paul Chapman.

Hart, O. (1995) *Firms, Contracts, and Financial Structure*. Oxford: Clarendon Press.

Hermalin, B.E and Weisbach, M.S. (2003) 'Boards of Directors as an endogenously determined institution: a survey of the economic literature', *FRBNY Economic Policy Review*, April: 7–26.

Hill, C.W.L. and Jones, T.M. (1992) 'Stakeholder-agency theory', *Journal of Management Studies*, Vol. 29, No. 2: 131–54.

Jensen, M.C. (2001) 'Value maximisation, stakeholder theory, and the corporate objective function', *European Financial Management*, Vol. 7, No. 3: 297–317.

Jensen, M.C. and Meckling, W.H. (1976) 'Theory of the firm: managerial behavior, agency costs and ownership structure', *Journal of Financial Economics*, Vol. 3: 305–60.

Kaptein, M. (2004) 'Business codes of multinational firms: what do they say?', *Journal of Business Ethics*, 50: 13–31.

Kay, J. and Silberston, A. (1995) 'Corporate governance', *National Institute Economic Review*, 84–97.

Letza, S., Sun, X. and Kirkbride, J. (2004) 'Shareholding versus stakeholding: a critical review of corporate governance', *Corporate Governance: An International Review*, Vol. 12, No. 3: 242–62.

Monks, R.A.G. and Minow, N. (2004) *Corporate Governance* (3rd edn). Oxford: Blackwell Publishing.

Shleifer, A. and Vishny, R.W. (1997) 'A survey of corporate governance', *Journal of Finance*, Vol. 52 (June), No. 2: 737–83.

Smith, A. (1937; first published, 1776) *The Wealth of Nations*. New York: Random House.

Solomon, J. and Solomon, A. (2004) *Corporate Governance and Accountability*. Chichester: Wiley.

Sternberg, E. (1997) 'The defects of stakeholder theory', *Corporate Governance: An International Review*, Vol. 5, No. 1: 3–10.

Vinten, G. (2001) 'Shareholder versus stakeholder – is there a governance dilemma?', *Corporate Governance: An International Review*, Vol. 9, No. 1: 36–47.

Corporate Governance Regulation

Stakeholders can gain information about a company's corporate governance practices from a variety of sources, including the annual report and accounts, professional journals, news media and web sites. Quoted companies are becoming increasingly aware that, as regards their annual report and accounts, public perceptions of corporate governance are an important concern as well as the financial results. The annual report and accounts now provide significantly more information about corporate governance than they did a decade ago, which is largely due to the increasing volume of recommendations, particularly those contained in *The Combined Code on Corporate Governance* (Financial Reporting Council, 2003). Directors of quoted companies are from time to time reminded of the need to pay as much attention to the corporate governance section of the annual report as they pay to presentation of the financial results.[1]

The aim of this chapter is to provide an overview of some of the codes and regulations designed to improve corporate governance. The major part of this chapter is devoted to UK corporate governance codes. However, since this book contains two chapters relating to US corporate governance examples – Enron and WorldCom – reference is also made to the Sarbanes–Oxley Act of 2002.

RECENT DEVELOPMENTS IN THE UK

Since 1991 there have been several reports on corporate governance issues in the UK. The first of these was the Committee on the Financial Aspects of Corporate Governance, which was set up in 1991 under the chairmanship of Sir Adrian Cadbury in response to some UK financial scandals of the 1980s. The Bank of Credit and Commerce International (BCCI) was forced to close by the Bank of England in July 1991, yet the auditors' report appeared to give little prior indication of the bank's precarious position. Another case concerned Robert Maxwell, who was responsible for theft from employee pension schemes under his control and whose business empire collapsed in December 1991. The preface to the report of the Cadbury Committee acknowledged 'the continuing concern about standards of financial reporting and accountability, heightened by BCCI, Maxwell and the controversy over directors' pay which has kept corporate governance in the public eye' (Cadbury Report, 1992: 9).

The Cadbury Report made a number of recommendations, many of which attempted to address what were seen as recent failures in corporate governance, where boards of directors had been dominated by particularly forceful chairmen and chief executives. For instance, the Cadbury Report recommended that quoted company boards should have a minimum of three non-executive directors, who should be 'independent' of the company, and they should be selected with the same impartiality and care as senior executives. In addition, the Cadbury Report recommended that quoted companies should have an audit committee, a nomination committee (to recommend board appointments) and a remuneration committee (to recommend the remuneration of executive directors). The membership of these committees should be wholly or mainly non-executive directors.

The Greenbury Committee was formed after widespread public concern over what were seen as excessive amounts of remuneration paid to directors of quoted companies and newly privatized companies. 'Recent concerns about executive remuneration have centred above all on some large pay increases and large gains from share options in the recently privatized utility industries. These increases have sometimes coincided with staff reductions, pay restraint for other staff and price increases . . . there have also been concerns about the amounts of compensation paid to some departing Directors' (Greenbury Report, 1995: 9).

The Greenbury Committee were keen to ensure that directors' remuneration was linked to company performance, and the committee did not seem to see a problem with high levels of pay *per se*, as long as they were justified on the basis of the company's financial results:

> A key concern should be to ensure, through the remuneration system, that directors share the interest of shareholders in making the company successful. Performance-related remuneration can be highly effective in aligning interest in this way. In many companies, therefore, there will be a case for a high gearing of performance-related to fixed pay. But there are two constraints on this. First, there will usually be a level of basic salary below which it will not be practicable to go. Second, the requirements and priorities of companies vary. The gearing which suits one company may be quite unsuitable for another. (Greenbury Report, 1995: 38)

The Greenbury Report also addressed the problem of departing directors whose performance had not been noticeably successful, but who still managed to leave the company with generous compensation for loss of office:

Compensation payments to Directors on loss of office have been a cause of public and shareholder concern in recent times. Criticism has been directed at the scale of some of the payments made and at their apparent lack of justification in terms of performance. Some payments have been described as 'rewards for failure'. (Greenbury Report, 1995: 45)

When the Greenbury Report was published in 1995 it dealt specifically with the question of directors' remuneration and many of its recommendations were developed from the earlier Cadbury Report. The Greenbury Report recommended that the remuneration committee should consist exclusively of non-executive directors (the Cadbury Report had recommended wholly or mainly non-executive directors). These non-executive directors should have no personal financial interest, no potential conflicts of interest arising from cross-directorships and no day-to-day involvement in running the business.

The Hampel Committee was created in 1995 to review implementation of the findings of the Cadbury and Greenbury Committees. The Hampel Committee published its report in 1998. Most of the recommendations in the earlier reports were then published in 1998 by the London Stock Exchange as *The Combined Code: Principles of Good Governance and Code of Best Practice*.

The Turnbull Report, *Internal Control: Guidance for Directors on the Combined Code* was published by the Internal Control Working Party of the Institute of Chartered Accountants in England and Wales in 1999 and provided guidance to directors on the internal control procedures seen as necessary to manage risk in organizations. Matters such as the identification, evaluation and management of risk are covered in the report, as well as the required disclosures in the annual report.

Next, the Higgs Review and the Smith Report were published in 2003. Derek Higgs had been commissioned by the UK government to review the role and effectiveness of non-executive directors, following financial scandals including Enron and WorldCom. Public confidence in non-executive directors had been eroded, for example, by reports that a third of non-executive directors are recruited through personal contacts (the 'old boy network') and that Lord Wakeham, a former UK government cabinet minister, sat on the boards of 16 companies including Enron.[2] The Higgs Review made a number of recommendations for *The Combined Code* to be revised, for instance enhancing the role of the senior independent director, detailing the role of the non-executive director and the duties of the nomination committee.

The Smith Report was also prompted by the Enron and WorldCom scandals, and the working party (appointed by the Financial Reporting Council) provided guidance on audit committees. Responsibility for reviewing and updating corporate governance recommendations was transferred from the London Stock Exchange to the Financial Reporting Council. In 2003 the Financial Reporting Council published *The Combined Code on*

Corporate Governance and this version incorporated revisions arising out of Turnbull, Smith and Higgs.

Some commentators have suggested that corporate governance tends to be reviewed only when a crisis presents itself. Such reviews represent special solutions to specific problems, rather than general solutions to the problems of corporate governance as a whole. Dewing and Russell (2000: 357) refer to the '*ad hoc* establishment of corporate governance committees in direct response to particular public concerns'. The Cadbury Committee was a direct response to public concerns over well-publicized corporate scandals and the Greenbury Committee was a direct response to public concern over what was seen as excessive remuneration taken by boards of directors of quoted companies. Interestingly, the Higgs Review and the Smith Report in the UK were commissioned directly as a result of the corporate collapse of Enron and WorldCom in the United States.

For those who saw business ethics as the essential issue to be addressed, the recommendations offered by bodies such as the Cadbury Committee did not seem to provide a solution. Thus, following the publication of the Cadbury Report, Boyd (1996: 177) argued that 'the question remains as to the best means of effecting cultural change in the boardroom, and in particular the role of the law in promoting responsible conduct. Most analysts are sceptical about the Cadbury Code of Best Conduct as an effective model for ethical corporate governance'.

One example of a cultural issue is the presence or absence of women on UK boards of directors. The Higgs Review was the first to draw attention to this issue, which had been ignored in previous reports. The low number of women directors in UK quoted companies was acknowledged in the Higgs Review, and boards were encouraged to 'draw more actively from areas . . . where women tend to be more strongly represented' (2003: 93). Although no specific recommendation was incorporated in the Financial Reporting Council's 2003 version of *The Combined Code on Corporate Governance,* it did adopt the Higgs suggestions for good practice and implicitly addressed the issue of gender imbalance on company boards. For example, on page 67 it stated that the nomination committee should: (a) 'evaluate the balance of skills, knowledge and experience on the board and, in the light of this evaluation, prepare a description of the role and capabilities required for a particular appointment'; (b) 'regularly review the structure, size and composition (including the skills, knowledge and experience) of the board and make recommendations to the board with regard to any changes'; and (c) 'consider candidates from a wide range of backgrounds and look beyond the "usual suspects"'. The Higgs Review also led to the Department of Trade and Industry commissioning a report on the recruitment and development of non-executive directors. The Tyson Report (2003) explicitly recommended diversity in board membership, particularly with regard to female participation.

THE SARBANES–OXLEY ACT

In 2002 Paul Sarbanes, a Democrat Senator, and Michael Oxley, a Republican Congressman, were responsible for a radical piece of corporate legislation, the Sarbanes–Oxley Act. This Act of Congress is regarded by many commentators as the single most important piece of legislation affecting companies since the Securities Exchange Act of 1934. In the USA, corporate crises associated with companies such as Enron, Tyco and Global Crossing seem to have hastened the introduction of the Sarbanes–Oxley legislation. There is some evidence that the bankruptcy of WorldCom on 21 July 2002, and the public outrage that followed, encouraged President G.W. Bush to sign into law nine days later the Sarbanes–Oxley legislation.[3]

The Sarbanes–Oxley Act introduces sweeping corporate law changes relating to financial reporting, internal accounting controls, personal loans from companies to their directors, whistleblowing and destruction of documents. In addition, Sarbanes–Oxley severely restricts the range of additional services that an audit firm can provide to a client. There are increased penalties for directors and professionals who have conspired to commit fraud. Some examples follow of its provisions.

Section 906 of the Act requires that all periodic reports containing financial statements filed with the SEC must be accompanied by a written statement by the chief executive officer (CEO) and chief financial officer (CFO) of the company, certifying that the report fully complies with the Securities Exchange Act and fairly presents, in all material respects, the financial condition and results of operations. The penalties for knowingly certifying a statement which does not comply with the requirements can be severe: up to $1 million in fines and/or up to ten years' imprisonment.

Section 1102 provides that 'knowing and willful' destruction of any record or document with intent to impair an official proceeding carries fines and/or imprisonment up to 20 years.

Section 806 provides protection for employees who provide evidence of fraud. There is also protection for 'whistleblowers' in publicly traded corporations. No company, officer or employee may threaten or harass an employee who reasonably believes that a criminal offence has been committed.

Section 501 of the legislation also aimed to promote rules to address conflicts of interest where analysts recommend securities when their companies are involved in investment banking activities.

The Sarbanes–Oxley legislation also established a Public Company Accounting Oversight Board (PCAOB) to be responsible to the Securities and Exchange Commission (SEC) for the regulation of auditing in US companies, inspection of accounting firms and disciplinary proceedings.

As a result of the Sarbanes–Oxley legislation, some companies felt that the burden of compliance was too high in relation to the perceived benefits. Companies were reported to be spending 'millions of dollars revamping their internal controls, updating compliance regimes, writing codes of ethics, setting up hotlines for internal complaints, writing governance principles and board committee charters. They are paying auditors and lawyers greater fees, as well as directors'.[4] The chief executive of the New York Stock Exchange (NYSE), John Thain, argued that the additional burden of compliance was dissuading foreign companies from listing on the NYSE.[5]

DISCUSSION

In October 2004 the UK Association of Chartered Certified Accountants (ACCA) reported the results of a survey of the largest 1,000 listed companies in the UK. It was reported that almost three-quarters of top directors believed that corporate governance compliance was taking up time that could more usefully be spent improving the company.[6] And the head of corporate governance at ACCA was quoted as saying that *The Combined Code on Corporate Governance* appeared to be turning into a box-ticking exercise. Thirty per cent of respondents to the survey said the main aim of corporate governance was to protect shareholders and another thirty per cent said the main aim was to optimize long-term wealth creation. The remainder ranked the two goals equally. One interpretation could be that the goal of optimizing long-term wealth creation would benefit all stakeholders, and not just shareholders. Nevertheless the results of the survey seem to suggest that directors of large quoted companies do see shareholders as an important stakeholder group, and probably the most important stakeholder group.

A year after *The Combined Code on Corporate Governance* was published, Derek Higgs – the author of the Higgs Review – was reported as being concerned that some companies had failed to embrace the spirit of the code, although he believed that the majority of companies were getting on with adapting to it.[7]

In the UK, companies were also faced with the prospect of additional reporting obligations as a result of a revised operating and financial review (OFR) statement. In 2004 the UK government proposed legislation for a comprehensive OFR, which would accompany the annual reports and accounts with the intention of allowing investors to make more informed judgements about a company's long-term prospects.[8]

The head of KPMG, Gene O'Kelly, was reportedly positive about the impact of the Sarbanes–Oxley legislation in the United States:

> Boards generally, and especially the independent directors who constitute audit committees, are taking seriously their heightened responsibilities as representatives of the shareholders. Audit committee meetings, once short briefings, now focus on reputational issues, transparency management. The law's effect on management behaviour is equally striking. Certifying financial statements on penalty of prison

time tends to focus a chief executive's mind, and chief executives are taking a deeper interest in their organization's financial reporting. Managements are reinvigorating their ethics policies and procedures.[9]

While the US legislation focuses on fines and imprisonment as sanctions to *deter fraudulent corporate behaviour*, the UK has to date emphasized codes of conduct which are less likely to incur criminal penalties. The UK *Combined Code on Corporate Governance* with its 'comply or explain' philosophy does not have the explicit backing of criminal penalties and seems to be designed instead to *encourage good corporate behaviour*.

A number of European Union companies have stock market listings in the United States and some of these companies have expressed concerns about the increased compliance costs they face as a result of the Sarbanes–Oxley legislation. Although convergence on corporate governance between the European Union and the United States is a future possibility, Greene and Boury (2004) argue that mutual recognition is unlikely in the short term:

> Europe may find itself in an increasingly defensive posture as it struggles to keep the long arm of the US federal government from dictating corporate governance policies to the many European companies that have accessed the US capital markets and cannot extract themselves without great difficulty. This trend would be regrettable, as it does not hold out the promise of substantial transatlantic convergence, but threatens continued European interest in participating in US markets. (Greene and Boury, 2004: 34)

However, no matter which codes and regulations are implemented, it is difficult to envisage a system which is completely free from the possibility of corporate governance failure. Clarke (2004: 160) argues that 'there will never be a "perfect" system of corporate governance. It is important that the most obvious abuses will be outlawed, and loopholes closed, but the ingenuity of self-interest will lead to the devising of new schemes to evade accountability'. Corporate governance regulation can claim to be successful if it encourages a business environment where warning signals are picked up early and appropriate action is taken quickly by the regulators. But in framing corporate governance codes and regulations, regulators need to strike a balance between too much regulation (which can inhibit wealth creation) and too little regulation (which can lead to corporate governance abuses).

REFERENCES

Boyd, C. (1996) 'Ethics and corporate governance: the issues raised by the Cadbury Report in the United Kingdom', *Journal of Business Ethics*, Vol. 15: 167–82.

Cadbury Report (1992) *Report of the Committee on the Financial Aspects of Corporate Governance*. London: Gee Publishing.

Clarke, T. (2004) 'Cycles of crisis and regulation: the enduring agency and stewardship problems of corporate governance', *Corporate Governance: An International Review*, Vol. 12, No. 2: 153–61.

Dewing, I.P. and Russell, P.O. (2000) 'Cadbury and beyond: perceptions on establishing a permanent body for corporate governance regulation', *British Accounting Review*, Vol. 32, No. 4: 355–74.

Financial Reporting Council (2003) *The Combined Code on Corporate Governance*. London: Financial Reporting Council.

Greenbury Report (1995) *Directors' Remuneration*. London: Gee Publishing.

Greene, E. and Boury, P. (2004) 'Post-Sarbanes–Oxley corporate governance in Europe and the USA: Americanisation or convergence?', *International Journal of Disclosure and Governance*, Vol. 1, No. 1: 21–34.

Hampel Report (1998) *Committee on Corporate Governance: Final Report*. London: Gee Publishing.

Higgs Review (2003) *Review of the Role and Effectiveness of Non-Executive Directors*. London: Department of Trade and Industry.

Lander, G.P. (2004) *What is Sarbanes–Oxley?* New York: McGraw-Hill.

London Stock Exchange (1998) *The Combined Code: Principles of Good Governance and Code of Best Practice*. London: London Stock Exchange.

Sarbanes–Oxley Act of 2002. *Public Law 107–204*. Washington, DC, 30 July.

Smith Report (2003) *Audit Committees: Combined Code Guidance*. London: Financial Reporting Council.

Stittle, J. (2003) *Annual Reports: Delivering Your Corporate Message to Stakeholders*. Aldershot: Gower.

Turnbull Report (1999) *Internal Control: Guidance for Directors on the Combined Code*. London: Institute of Chartered Accountants in England and Wales.

Tyson, L. (2003) *The Tyson Report on the Recruitment and Development of Non-Executive Directors*. London: London Business School.

NOTES

1 See, for instance, Stittle, 2003: 135–60.

2 *Financial Times*, 27 April 2002: 14.

3 *New York Times*, 2 August 2002: 1.

4 *Financial Times*, 14 June 2004: 26.

5 *Financial Times*, 14 June 2004: 26.

6 *Financial Times*, 11 October 2004: 3.

7 *Financial Times*, 19 October 2004: 6

8 See *Accountancy*, June 2004: 29–33.

9 *Financial Times*, 30 July 2004: 19.

Maxwell

In November 1991 the UK business scene was stunned to learn that Robert Maxwell, an apparently successful business leader with important newspaper and publishing interests, had disappeared at sea from his yacht *Lady Ghislaine*. In the following weeks it became clear that his business empire was in serious financial difficulties, and had been for some time. A report published by the Department of Trade and Industry (DTI) in March 2001 was referred to in one newspaper[1] as describing 'a tale of greed, cliquiness, naivety and amateurism at the heart of Europe's leading financial centre'. The DTI inspectors concluded that 'the chief culprits in the deception that allowed the publisher to raid £400m from the pension fund of Mirror Group Newspapers were Maxwell and his son, Kevin'.[2]

Robert Maxwell was originally born Jan Ludvik Hoch in 1923. His father was a labourer and the family apparently lived in poverty in a small village in what was then Czechoslovakia. Maxwell found it easy to learn languages and he claimed to be able to speak nine, including Czech, French, German and Russian, as well as English. Given that he had been born into a Jewish family, he was lucky to escape from mainland Europe in 1940. Many members of his immediate family were to die later in the Holocaust. There are differing accounts of how he managed to reach Britain; what is known is that in May 1940 he arrived in Liverpool, having travelled by ship from Marseille in France.

Whilst in the UK Maxwell perfected his English, and acquired English customs and mannerisms. Maxwell had an eventful war, being promoted eventually to captain in 1945. After fighting in France, he was awarded the Military Cross for exceptional bravery by Field Marshal Montgomery. The name Jan Ludvik Hoch was dropped in favour of the name Robert Maxwell and he married Elisabeth Meynard. At the end of the war, Maxwell was stationed in Berlin where the army made good use of his linguistic abilities.

MAXWELL'S EARLY BUSINESS AND POLITICAL AFFAIRS

Maxwell was ambitious to succeed in the publishing industry and became involved in a number of business ventures. In May 1951 he raised the finance to purchase from Butterworths their share of a publishing company which he renamed Pergamon Press, and with which he was to be associated for the rest of his life. During the 1950s and 1960s Maxwell built up Pergamon Press into a successful publisher of books and journals, particularly scientific journals.

Maxwell was keen to succeed in political life as well as in business. He was adopted as the Labour Party candidate for North Buckinghamshire and in the 1964 general election was elected to Parliament. While there, Maxwell attempted to pursue both a political career and a business career but he appeared to find it difficult to reconcile his business interests with his publicly stated socialist principles. By 1964 he was already a millionaire and was distrusted by some Labour Party members. When speaking to a Labour Party conference in 1967 he tried to justify sending some of his children to public schools (Bower, 1992: 125), a point of view which did not endear him to Labour Party activists. In July 1964, Pergamon Press was floated on the London Stock Exchange. Maxwell's stake in Pergamon was estimated at approximately £10m, although his actual wealth was probably greater since at that time some of his wealth was also held in trusts in Liechtenstein.

In 1968 Maxwell became involved in a bid for the *News of the World*, a UK Sunday newspaper. A bitterly contested takeover battle ensued when Rupert Murdoch, an Australian publisher, decided to bid for the newspaper. By early 1969 Maxwell had to concede defeat and Murdoch acquired control. Also in 1969, Maxwell wanted to gain control of *The Sun*, a UK daily newspaper, but once again he lost out to his rival Rupert Murdoch. Maxwell believed that he was an innocent victim of the City establishment and his failed takeover bids only served to strengthen that belief. Maxwell and Murdoch were to remain rivals for the next two decades.

THE LEASCO PERGAMON TAKEOVER

The year 1969 was critical in Maxwell's career. He and an American, Saul Steinberg (head of Leasco), agreed to merge their businesses, with Leasco purchasing Pergamon Press and Maxwell accepting a subordinate role in the combined enterprise. Steinberg had been very successful in the United States in the business of leasing computers. The intention was to pool the expertise and resources of Steinberg and Maxwell by storing the data contained in Maxwell's scientific journals and books on computers. In 1969 this was a radical and visionary proposal.

Maxwell had been trying to grow his business empire, with Pergamon as the basis. His strategy was to attempt to take over companies such as the *News of the World* and increase their profitability and hence market value, so his defeat in the battle for the *News of the World* was a considerable blow to his business ambitions. According to Bower (1992), Leasco's profits in 1968 were $27m and assets amounted to $1bn. Steinberg had been successful in a number of takeovers and mergers and was still only 29 years old. For Maxwell it was important that the accounts of Pergamon for 1968 should show a substantial profit since this would support the share price and assist his negotiations with Leasco. The auditors of Pergamon were Chalmers Impey, but the *Sunday Times* had questioned the audit procedures used by Chalmers Impey on Pergamon's accounts, for instance, alleging that stocks were overvalued.

In June 1969 Leasco and Pergamon had reached agreement in principle that Leasco would bid for Pergamon after having successfully completed investigations into the financial affairs of Pergamon. However, Leasco's financial advisers were finding it difficult to extract the necessary information from Pergamon and were finding it difficult to receive answers to their questions from Maxwell. By August 1969 Steinberg and his advisers had doubts about the future profitability of Pergamon; they were becoming increasingly nervous about the takeover and wanted to withdraw from the bid. However, since Leasco had agreed to the takeover in principle, a valid reason to withdraw would be required. So Steinberg wanted to withdraw from the bid, but Maxwell wanted the bid to proceed.

The Takeover Panel had to decide whether Leasco could be allowed to withdraw their bid for Pergamon. It was finally agreed that the bid would go ahead. Maxwell would remain as chairman of Pergamon but would not be managing director. The Takeover Panel also called for a full Board of Trade inquiry into the circumstances surrounding the Leasco bid for Pergamon.

The two inspectors appointed by the Board of Trade were a lawyer, Owen Stable QC, and an accountant, Ronald Leach, who was a senior partner in Peat Marwick Mitchell. At the same time the accountants Price Waterhouse carried out an independent audit of Pergamon's 1968 financial statements. The Price Waterhouse audit was carried out by a senior partner, Martin Harris, and among its conclusions was the finding that the reported profits of Pergamon for 1968 had been overstated. Instead of a profit of £2.1m the corrected figure would have been £140,000. This represented a huge reduction and it caused some consternation among the public that two different firms of accountants could arrive at such different conclusions about Pergamon's profits.

Chalmers Impey subsequently resigned as auditors and Cooper Brothers took over the audit. No doubt there was some understandable confusion amongst non-accountants over the distinction between 'cash' and 'profit' and the subjectivity involved in calculating a firm's 'profit', especially when different firms of accountants used different assumptions. Nevertheless, episodes such as the Price Waterhouse report were instrumental in the accounting profession deciding to confront the issue of uniform accounting standards. This resulted in the setting up of the Accounting Standards Committee (subsequently renamed the Accounting Standards Board).

The accounting profession was concerned that it would lose credibility, and even worse, invite government intervention, if it did not try to impose some minimum standards for consistent financial reporting treatments. There is little doubt that the accounting profession in the UK (and in the USA) wanted to retain as far as possible its independence from state intervention in terms of accounting and auditing.

Following publication of the Price Waterhouse report, Leasco were understandably reluctant to pursue the takeover of Pergamon, given the restatement of Pergamon's reported profits and assets and the reduced valuation placed on its stocks. In fact Maxwell was eventually able in 1974 to regain control of Pergamon. But one of the greatest blows to Maxwell came from the inspectors who had been appointed in 1969 by the Board of Trade (subsequently renamed the Department of Trade and Industry, or DTI).

The DTI report was published in July 1971 and among the conclusions of the inspectors, Stable and Leach, was the following critical statement:

> We are also convinced that Mr Maxwell regarded his stewardship duties fulfilled by showing the maximum profits which any transaction could be devised to show. Furthermore, in reporting to shareholders and investors he had a reckless and unjustified optimism which enabled him on some occasions to disregard unpalatable facts and on others to state what he must have known to be untrue ... We regret having to conclude that, notwithstanding Mr Maxwell's acknowledged abilities and energy, he is not in our opinion a person who can be relied on to exercise proper stewardship of a publicly quoted company. (Bower, 1992: 286–7)

The phrase 'not in our opinion a person who can be relied on to exercise proper stewardship of a publicly quoted company' was to haunt Maxwell for the rest of his life.

Maxwell did attempt to argue through the courts that the inspectors had not given him a fair hearing and had not properly consulted him about the report's conclusions. But his appeal was not successful. Where many people would have simply accepted a reduced role in business life from that point, Maxwell instead was determined that he would not be beaten by the 'Establishment', even though the DTI inspectors produced two further reports in April 1972 and November 1973, which were also damning of Maxwell's business methods.

AFTER THE LEASCO PERGAMON TAKEOVER

Maxwell was legendary for his attempts to settle disputes through the courts and he began many legal actions against his business rivals as well as against journalists who attempted to report on his business activities. For instance, Davies (1993: 304) refers to Maxwell's 'litigious reputation'. It is quite possible that the fear of being sued in the courts made journalists (especially financial journalists) and financial analysts reluctant to write critically in public about Maxwell and his business affairs. When Maxwell learned in 1987 that Tom Bower was about to publish a biography, *Maxwell: The Outsider*, he issued twelve writs against Bower and his publishers and also instructed a Mirror journalist, Joe Haines, to write an 'authorized' biography (Bower, 1992: 1–2).

Meanwile, in a bid to gain acceptance at a business and political level, Maxwell took great care to cultivate relationships with world leaders and was particularly keen to be seen with political leaders on the world stage. Haines (1988) reproduces a wealth of evidence showing Maxwell meeting political leaders such as Mikhail Gorbachev of the Soviet Union, President Mitterrand of France, President Reagan of the USA and Prime Minister Margaret Thatcher of the UK.

In 1974, when Maxwell eventually regained control of Pergamon, he put his energies into building up the business. This he managed to do successfully. By 1977 Pergamon had substantially increased its assets and reported profits. Maxwell was keen to expand his business interests and in 1980 turned his attention to the British Printing Corporation (BPC), later renamed the British Printing and Communications Corporation (BPCC). BPC had been earning relatively low profits and Maxwell believed he could transform the company into an efficient organization. He began to buy up shares in BPC but was faced with opposition from the board of BPC and its chairman and managing director, Peter Robinson. In February 1981 Maxwell gained control and became deputy chairman and chief executive. Maxwell then struggled to turn the company around.

In the early 1980s it was generally recognized that printing companies in the UK were overstaffed and that restrictive practices were hindering efficient production. At one printing press, the Park Royal plant in West London:

> Six men instead of one were 'minding' machines and if one of those six was absent through illness, the management were compelled to hire a temporary replacement with enormous penalty costs. Even seventy-year-olds were still on the payroll, although they were not working. Maxwell seized on these symbols to undermine the unions and humiliate Robinson's record. (Bower, 1992: 343)

Maxwell clearly believed that he was the person to change these practices. He had possibly been impressed by Rupert Murdoch's own bold decision some years earlier to bypass the trade unions and move his printing presses to Wapping in East London. Whereas Peter Robinson had been attempting to make efficiency gains at BPC at a more sedate pace that would not upset the unions, Maxwell instead used a combination of aggression and charm:

> In the first five years of Maxwell's reign, very few of the company's directors, even those whom he appointed, survived for more than one year. Few could satisfy his demands or cope with the stress. 'It was annoying and mentally tiring', recalls David Perry, . . . 'that he acted without consulting anyone'. (Bower, 1992: 346)

Nicholas Davies, who worked for Maxwell for a number of years, wrote of Maxwell's relationship with the trade unions:

> After months of wrangling and hard-fought battles, union leader Bill Keys commented: 'Maxwell is the greatest wheeler-dealer we've ever met . . . a man who can charm the birds off the trees and then shoot them'. (Davies, 1993: 33)

Maxwell improved the finances of BPC and carried out a major programme of investment in up-to-date machinery. During the early 1980s, with both Pergamon and BPC making healthy profits, Maxwell could validly claim to be a successful entrepreneur, with the DTI reports a decade or more behind him. Despite the fact that Rupert Murdoch had prevented him from taking over the *News of the World*, and subsequently *The Sun*, Maxwell was still ambitious to gain a reputation as a newspaper proprietor.

During the first half of the 1980s, Maxwell continued to take over some companies and take minority stakes in others. However, it was not always clear where the ultimate ownership of these companies lay. Maxwell had devised an extremely complicated corporate structure for the companies under his control, with shareholdings spread among the Maxwell Foundation, his own and family shareholdings, the Maxwell Charitable Trust and trusts based in Liechtenstein. Attempting to unravel this complex ownership structure was a massive task. Figure 1 attempts to illustrate the intricate pattern of private companies, trusts and quoted companies which made up the 'Maxwell empire' in 1991. But even this cannot fully capture the labyrinthine structure of the organization, which was reputed to include 400 private companies.

In 1984 Maxwell finally achieved his ambition of controlling a major UK newspaper, Mirror Group Newspapers, which published the *Daily Mirror* and *Sunday Mirror*. Unlike much of the British press, the *Daily Mirror* could normally be counted on as a friend of the Labour Party, especially during general elections. There was therefore some concern in the Labour Party when it was learned that Maxwell, even though he had

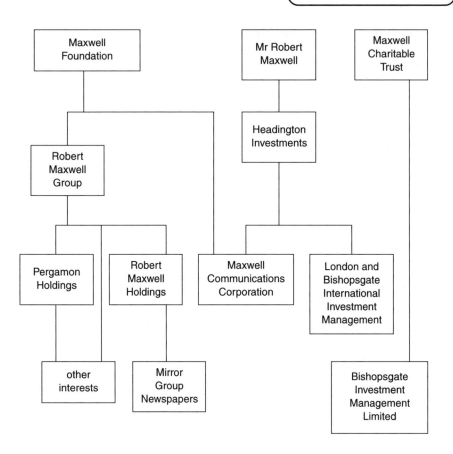

Figure 1 Maxwell Organization in 1991

Source: Adapted from *Financial Times*, 31 March 2001: 7

himself been a Labour member of parliament, was interested in acquiring the newspaper. Nevertheless, Reed International was keen to sell the newspaper and Mirror Group Newspapers was acquired for £90m. Three journalists on the *Mirror* who had left-wing leanings and expected to be fired were Paul Foot, Joe Haines and Geoffrey Goodman. However they apparently secured assurances that Maxwell would not interfere in their journalism, and they wrote for the *Mirror* for a number of years.

During the second half of the 1980s, Maxwell made numerous attempts to control or buy stakes in companies engaged mainly in publishing, television and information services, but also in other areas such as stores and banking. These purchases and sales of shareholdings involved dozens of companies. In 1987 Maxwell bid unsuccessfully for the US publisher Harcourt Brace Jovanovich, but in the following year he bought the US publishers Macmillan for $2.6bn. In 1987 BPCC was renamed Maxwell Communications Corporation (MCC).

THE FINAL MONTHS

Then, in 1991, Maxwell bid for the New York newspaper the *Daily News*. A dispute with the unions had adversely affected profitability at the newspaper and the owners, the Chicago Tribune Group, were keen to sell the newspaper. Maxwell was himself keen to add the *Daily News* to his publishing interests and he seems to have assumed that he could turn round the newspaper's fortunes in the same way that he had done with BPCC and Pergamon. However, he had had mixed results with the Mirror Group newspapers and circulation had fallen, while circulation figures for its main rival (*The Sun,* owned by Rupert Murdoch) had increased. The *Daily News*, due to continuing disputes with the trade unions, proved to be a considerable problem for Maxwell and a drain on his group's resources.

In March 1991, Pergamon was sold to the Dutch group Elsevier for £440m. It appeared that Maxwell's group of companies was beginning to run short of cash. The sale of Pergamon, supposedly a fundamental part of the Maxwell business empire, led to speculation about Maxwell's financial difficulties. During this period Maxwell was also pledging shares in MCC as collateral for loans. What was later to become apparent was that Maxwell's cash requirements were leading to a steady increase in indebtedness. But what only became clear later on was that Maxwell was also pledging shares in company pension funds as collateral for further loans. Why had the pension fund trustees not objected to this? In the case of MGN, Maxwell had removed the trade unionists from the pension fund and replaced them with his sons, Kevin and Ian Maxwell. Management of most of the pension fund was given over to the Maxwell-controlled company Bishopsgate Investment Management Limited, which had taken the decision to invest in Maxwell-owned companies such as MCC.

One of the basic principles of pension trusteeship is that the pension fund should be treated as an entity separate and distinct from the company that employs the workers who contribute to the pension fund. It is of paramount importance that the trustees should be sufficiently independent to be able to object to the improper use of pension fund assets. Otherwise there is a real danger that the managers of the company will attempt to use the pension fund as a source of cheap finance. In addition, it is important that there is a separation of the risks of the company and the pension fund. For instance, it is unwise for a pension fund to invest a large proportion of its assets in the related company. For, if the company goes into liquidation, the pension fund assets are likely to be worthless. What the members of the pension fund need is some assurance that, even if their employer goes into liquidation, their retirement pensions are still protected.

However, Maxwell had managed in a fairly crude way to get round the pension fund rules, which had been designed to ensure independence. When Maxwell purchased Mirror Group Newspapers (MGN) in 1984, the pension fund had a substantial surplus. Maxwell took advantage of the regulations that allowed the employer effectively to take a holiday from making employer's contributions. This was effectively the same as MGN receiving a cash windfall. Consequently the surplus diminished. Maxwell was also able to raid the assets of the pension fund by pledging their shares as collateral against loans he was raising with the banks. Although Maxwell had been successful with BPCC and Pergamon, he had been less successful in other areas. In 1991 the share price of MCC and MGN began to fall. MGN had been floated in May 1991, although the flotation had not been particularly successful.

MGN and MCC shares were pledged as collateral for further loans and Maxwell's companies became increasingly indebted during 1991. Towards the end of 1991 the share price of MCC began to decline. Goldman Sachs began pressing Maxwell for repayment of overdue loans which amounted to £80m. Goldman Sachs also began selling their holdings of MCC shares, which had the effect of decreasing the share price even further. There was a danger that shares held as collateral would also be sold, leading to a vicious downward spiral of share sales leading to a falling share price, in turn provoking further share sales. In New York, Citibank were also beginning to sell shares held as collateral, on the grounds that loans were not being repaid.

Towards the end of October 1991, Maxwell must have been aware of the effect that impending sales of shares would have on the share price. On 31 October 1991, Maxwell left the Mirror building and flew by helicopter to Luton; from there he was flown in his company jet to Gibraltar, where the captain and crew of his yacht, the *Lady Ghislaine*, were waiting. Maxwell sailed first to Madeira and then on to Tenerife. The yacht arrived at Los Cristianos in Gran Canaria on the morning of Tuesday 5 November. It was discovered shortly after arriving at Los Cristianos that Maxwell was not on board and must have disappeared overboard on the last leg of the trip.

When Kevin Maxwell and Ian Maxwell were informed of their father's disappearance at sea, they requested the Stock Exchange in London to suspend dealing in MCC and MGN shares. The Stock Exchange at first seemed reluctant to suspend trading in the shares simply because the chairman was missing. But as news of the disappearance leaked to the market, the share price of MCC and MGN began to fall. The Stock Exchange then decided on the afternoon of 5 November to suspend trading in MCC and MGN shares. Ian Maxwell was appointed acting chairman of MGN and Kevin Maxwell was appointed as acting chairman of MCC.

Following a search at sea, Robert Maxwell's body was shortly afterwards recovered. The Spanish authorities seemed to conclude that Maxwell's death was simply an accident, although there has subsequently been speculation about the possibility of suicide. Maxwell was buried in Israel and speculation began to surface about the possibility that he had been murdered by Mossad, the Israeli Secret Service. This story was supported by two *Mirror* journalists, Gordon Thomas and Martin Dillon, whose book *The Assassination of Robert Maxwell: Israel's Superspy* was published in 2002. And in November 2003, Geoffrey Goodman, a former *Mirror* journalist, was reported[3] as supporting the theory that Maxwell had been murdered. It is certainly true that during his lifetime Robert Maxwell was an enigmatic figure, and no doubt speculation will continue about the true cause of his death.

When news of his death was announced, the *Daily Mirror* referred to him as the 'man who saved the *Mirror*' (Davies, 1993: 341), although other newspapers were less charitable. But towards the end of November 1991, the truth about Maxwell's business practices and methods, and the indebtedness of the companies with which he was involved, began to emerge. Debts of the Maxwell private companies were estimated at approximately £1bn. In addition, it was found that a substantial proportion of the Mirror pension fund investments had disappeared, for two reasons. Firstly, pension fund shares had been pledged as collateral for additional loans taken out by Maxwell. Secondly, some of the pension fund assets of MGN had been invested in MGN and MCC, whose share prices had fallen drastically.

It also emerged that some analysts, who had tried to warn of Maxwell's activities, had been subjected to threats of legal action. Derek Terrington, an analyst with Phillips and Drew wrote a sell notice on MCC shares in 1989. As a result Maxwell withdrew £80 million of the MCC pension fund from Phillips and Drew Fund Management and made a point of saying that it was due to Terrington's criticisms. Other analysts decided against publishing critical comments and instead informed their clients by word of mouth. According to Brian Sturgess, an analyst at BZW, 'since the criticism was done discreetly by phone and lunches, it was only the big institutions who got this information. All the other shareholders were left out'.[4]

In December 1991, Ian Maxwell and Kevin Maxwell were investigated by the Serious Fraud Office and both resigned from MGN and MCC. The *Daily Mirror* by now had completely reversed its original opinion of Maxwell as saviour of MGN, describing instead the fraud perpetrated by Robert Maxwell on MGN. With the revelation that something like 30,000 pensioners (Davies, 1993: 41) had badly lost out as a result of the Maxwell fraud, public sentiment turned against Maxwell.

In those last few days before he died Maxwell was still furiously borrowing money from banks, 'borrowing' money from the *Daily Mirror*, acting, as always, as if he owned everything and he had the absolute right to do as he wished with any of the companies, public or private, of which he held the stewardship. He had never changed; he had never learned. To the last, Maxwell was as guilty as the DTI reports of the 1970s had reported. (Davies, 1993: 332)

DISCUSSION

Smith (1992: 10–12) outlines four methods by which Maxwell was able to misappropriate funds from the companies under his control. Firstly, he pledged assets as security for additional loans. However, instead of delivering the assets to the lender, Maxwell would in some cases simply sell the assets for cash. For example, Berlitz language school was supposedly sold to a Japanese publishing company, but the shares had previously been pledged as security for loans from Swiss Volksbank and Lehman Brothers.

Secondly, he diverted shares and cash from Mirror Group Newspapers to Bishopsgate Investment Management Limited (controlled by Maxwell). The shares were then pledged as security for further loans to Maxwell's private companies.

Thirdly, Maxwell used cash gained from pledging shares to support the share price of MCC and MGN. These purchases were not disclosed, as they should have been under Stock Exchange regulations. Maxwell needed a relatively high share price to maintain his financial credibility with the banks who were lending to him. Maxwell also supported the share price of MCC by selling put options to Goldman Sachs with a strike price higher than that ruling in the market when the option was written. In other words, Goldman Sachs could immediately buy shares at the (lower) current market price, knowing that they would be guaranteed a profit when they later sold the shares to Maxwell at the higher price specified in the option.

Fourthly and most simply, Maxwell took cash from MGN. After the flotation of MGN, £43m was passed to Maxwell's private companies. Given the scale of what happened in the Maxwell organization, it was natural that the public would want to know who should be held accountable. The Department of Trade and Industry Report on events at Mirror Group Newspapers plc was published in March 2001 (DTI, 2001).

The DTI Report stated that it was clear to many people who dealt with Robert Maxwell that 'he was a bully and a domineering personality, but could be charming on occasions' (DTI, 2001: 319). Primary responsibility rested with Maxwell himself, but 'Kevin Maxwell gave very substantial assistance to Robert Maxwell and bears a heavy responsibility'.[5] Also, 'Ian Maxwell signed many documents without considering their implications and failed to carry out all the duties he had undertaken as a director of Bishopsgate Investment Management Limited'.[6]

The 2001 DTI report also cast considerable blame on the City of London institutions that had helped support Maxwell.[7] The accountants Coopers and Lybrand Deloitte bore a major responsibility for failing to report pension fund abuses to trustees.[8] The report also concluded that Maxwell bore 'the primary responsibility for manipulating the market in MCC shares and he did this because he was obsessed with the share price which to his mind reflected on his personal standing'.[9] However, Goldman Sachs also bore substantial responsibility for manipulation of the MCC share price.[10]

Other criticisms of the way MGN was run included the fact that Robert Maxwell was executive chairman and the independent directors had not been effective in exercising control over the chairman. The 2001 DTI Report included a telling section on Robert Maxwell's attitude to non-executive directors:

> Robert Maxwell had not reacted favourably in 1988 when he had been told that non-executive directors had to be appointed, but had eventually agreed that it was essential. However, Kevin Maxwell told us that Robert Maxwell was quite happy to have non-executives on the board; he had had a policy of having 'luminaries' on boards for some years. He had given jobs to former ministers, politicians and officials, as he had seen this as a way of exercising power in the Labour Party and helping friends who had lost office. Robert Maxwell also saw them as lending their name to the company just as distinguished scientists lent their name to his scientific journals by becoming members of the editorial boards of the journals. However, beyond that, non-executive directors had no function in Robert Maxwell's world. (DTI, 2001: 185–6)

Kevin Maxwell and Ian Maxwell were arrested on 18 June 1992 by London police working with the Serious Fraud Office (SFO).[11] They were charged with conspiracy to defraud, but were cleared in 1996. In the meantime, Kevin Maxwell was reputed to be Britain's biggest bankrupt in 1992, at the age of 33, after admitting debts of £400m.[12] Coopers and Lybrand Deloitte and some of their partners were disciplined by the Joint Disciplinary Scheme. Goldman Sachs was disciplined by their regulatory organization, the Securities and Futures Authority (SFA) and also contributed to a substantial settlement with the pension schemes without admission of liability.[13]

PricewaterhouseCoopers (PwC, the successor firm to Coopers and Lybrand) was reported in 2001 as saying that it had accepted the criticisms made in the DTI report and that it had made significant internal changes since the scandal had been revealed. Apart from potential damage to its reputation, PwC paid a Joint Disciplinary Scheme fine of £3.5m, contributed an undisclosed sum to the defrauded pension funds and paid liquidators £68m in an out-of-court settlement.[14] It was also reported that other city institutions (for instance the banks and financial advisers who acted for Maxwell) claimed that 'it was impossible to legislate further for, or provide more corporate governance against, crooked executive chairmen if directors don't stop them'.[15]

The Cadbury Committee, which reported in 1992, acknowledged that recent financial scandals (the Maxwell case was specifically referred to) were one of the reasons for the committee being asked to report on corporate governance matters. The Cadbury Committee made a number of recommendations (Cadbury Report, 1992: 58), some of which seem directly relevant to the Maxwell case:

There should be a clearly accepted division of responsibilities at the head of a company, which will ensure a balance of power and authority, such that no one individual has unfettered powers of decision. Where the chairman is also the chief executive, it is essential that there should be a strong and independent element on the board, with a recognised senior member. (Code of Best Practice, item 1.2)

The board should include non-executive directors of sufficient calibre and number for their views to carry significant weight in the board's decisions. (Code of Best Practice, item 1.3)

Non-executive directors should bring an independent judgement to bear on issues of strategy, performance, resources, including key appointments, and standards of conduct. (Code of Best Practice, item 2.1).

The majority [of non-executive directors] should be independent of management and free from any business or other relationship which could materially interfere with the exercise of their independent judgement. (Code of Best Practice, item 2.2)

However, the Cadbury Committee also appeared to accept that regulation on its own would never be sufficient to ensure 'good' corporate governance:

Had a Code such as ours been in existence in the past, we believe that a number of the recent examples of unexpected company failures and cases of fraud would have received attention earlier. It must, however, be recognised that no system of control can eliminate the risk of fraud without so shackling companies as to impede their ability to compete in the market place. (Cadbury Report, 1992: 12)

Effectively, the Cadbury Report is saying that in the final analysis a balance has to be struck to ensure an adequate level of corporate governance without stifling the play of competitive forces and entrepreneurship which are fundamental to a market-based economy.

Could the circumstances of the Maxwell collapse reasonably have been foreseen by those either in the City or ordinary investors? There is some evidence that some city analysts were aware of what was going on and some institutional investors were fortunate to receive and act on their discreet warnings. Individual investors were less lucky. Apart from the blunt warnings contained in the DTI reports of the early 1970s, there were some courageous journalists who were prepared to confront Maxwell's famous reputation for litigation. Roger Cowe[16] – writing in *The Guardian* in 1990 – argued that Robert Maxwell was striving to avoid joining the list of debt-bound businesses whose extraordinary growth during the 1980s was in danger of being followed by dramatic collapse in the 1990s. Cowe also referred to the dangers inherent in companies with chairmen who were in a position to dominate their boards of directors. His article was particularly timely given that the Maxwell empire was destined to collapse just over one year later. So it seems that there were some warnings around for those who cared to look for them.

Table 4.1 *Robert Maxwell: key events*

1923	Maxwell is born as Jan Ludvik Hoch in Czechoslovakia
1940	Arrives in Liverpool from Marseille, France
1945	Changes name to Robert Maxwell and marries Elisabeth Meynard
1951	Pergamon Press is established, publishing scientific journals and books
1964	Elected as a Labour MP for North Buckinghamshire; Pergamon Press is floated on London Stock Exchange
1969	Maxwell is unsuccessful in his bid for *News of The World* (Sunday newspaper); Maxwell attempts sale of Pergamon to Leasco
1970	Loses parliamentary seat in 1970 general election
1971	DTI Inspectors' critical report
1974	Regains control of Pergamon
1981	Gains control of British Printing Corporation (BPC), later renamed British Printing and Communications Corporation (BPCC)
1984	Purchases Mirror Group Newspapers
1987	Bids unsuccessfully for US publishers Harcourt Brace Jovanovich; BPCC is renamed Maxwell Communications Corporation (MCC)
1988	Purchases US publishers Macmillan at cost of $2.6bn
1991	Purchases *New York Daily News* newspaper (March); Mirror Group Newspapers (MGN) floated on London Stock Exchange (May); Maxwell disappears at sea from his yacht *Lady Ghislaine* (November); Maxwell's business empire collapses (December)
2001	DTI report into Mirror Group Newspapers

Discussion questions

1 Do you believe that, following the DTI reports of the early 1970s, the City should have been more sceptical of Maxwell's business activities?

2 Contrast Robert Maxwell's view of the role of the board of directors and the role of the non-executive director with recent guidance on corporate governance.

3 What do you believe are the main lessons that can be drawn from the failure of Maxwell's business empire?

4 Who were the main losers when the Maxwell empire crashed?

5 Is it likely that problems of the type and scale of Maxwell's financial dealings could be repeated in a quoted company in future?

REFERENCES

Bower, T. (1992) *Maxwell: The Outsider.* London: BCA.

Bower, T. (1996) *Maxwell: The Final Verdict.* London: HarperCollins.

Cadbury Report (1992) *Report of the Committee on the Financial Aspects of Corporate Governance.* London: Gee Publishing.

Davies, N. (1993) *The Unknown Maxwell.* London: Pan Books.

Department of Trade and Industry (2001) *Mirror Group Newspapers plc.* London: DTI.

Haines, J. (1988) *Maxwell.* London: Macdonald.

Smith, T. (1992) *Accounting for Growth.* London: Century Business.

NOTES

1 *Financial Times*, 31 March 2001: 6.

2 *Financial Times*, 31 March 2001: 6.

3 *Guardian*, 24 November 2003.

4 *Independent on Sunday*, 22 December 1991: 5.

5 DTI, 2001: 321.

6 DTI, 2001: 324.

7 See *Financial Times*, 31 March 2001: 6-7.

8 DTI, 2001: 324.

9 DTI, 2001: 357.

10 DTI, 2001: 358.

11 *Economist*, 20 June 1992: 93.

12 *Financial Times*, 27 August 2004.

13 See DTI, 2001: 318.

14 *Accountancy*, May 2001: 9.

15 *Accountancy*, May 2001: 9.

16 *Guardian*, 2 October 1990.

Polly Peck

In October 1990, Polly Peck, a large UK quoted company, was placed into administration. At the beginning of August 1990 the share price had stood at 418p, but by 20 September 1990 it had fallen to 108p. This represented a loss of nearly 75 per cent of their value in under two months. At this point, trading in the shares was suspended by the London Stock Exchange and Polly Peck collapsed with debts estimated at £1.3bn.

The Serious Fraud Office (SFO) prepared a case against Asil Nadir, chairman and chief executive, accusing him of theft and false accounting, but before the trial could get under way Asil Nadir dramatically fled the UK in 1993 for the comparative safety of northern Cyprus. It seems that, until the legal process is finally completed, many of the questions relating to Polly Peck will remain unanswered.

ASIL NADIR'S EARLY LIFE

Asil Nadir was born in May 1941 in Cyprus to a Turkish Cypriot family. In 1959 the Nadir family emigrated to London, but the connection with Cyprus was to be highly significant for Nadir's later business fortunes. At that time Cyprus faced increasing disputes between Greek and Turkish Cypriots. The move to London was well judged since violence erupted soon after and lasted for a number of years. In 1974 the northern part of Cyprus was invaded by the Turkish army, following an attempt by the terrorist organization EOKA to have Cyprus annexed to Greece. Although the invasion did improve security for the Turkish Cypriots, their new administration was not internationally recognized. Much of the property in northern Cyprus was owned by Greek Cypriots and this property (for example citrus trees and hotels) fell into disrepair, since the owners could not return to manage it. This has not helped northern Cyprus to develop economically.

Not long after arriving in London, Asil Nadir travelled to Turkey to study economics at university in Istanbul. He did not complete his studies, but married Aysegul and returned to London. Asil Nadir joined the family business and set up a clothing company called Wearwell. Despite fierce competition, Wearwell prospered under Nadir's management and branches were opened outside London. There seems little doubt that Asil Nadir was a charismatic and hard-working businessman and Hindle (1993) describes him as a workaholic. Wearwell was floated on the London Stock Exchange in 1973 and in the late 1970s began to export. Part of its operations involved sending material to northern Cyprus, where it could be machined and sewn at a lower cost than in the UK.

POLLY PECK'S EARLY YEARS

In 1980 Restro Investments, a private company controlled by Nadir and based in the tax haven of Jersey, made a cash offer for Polly Peck, a small company which had been quoted on the London Stock Exchange for a number of years. Polly Peck was also in the clothing industry, but its profitability had not been remarkable. Restro Investments acquired 58 per cent of the share capital of Polly Peck at a cost of £270,000. Over the next ten years, Polly Peck was to experience unprecedented growth under Nadir's management, so that ten years later that 58 per cent share of Polly Peck was worth just over £1bn (Hindle , 1993: 36). Small wonder then that shareholders who remained loyal to Polly Peck during the first half of the 1980s were so positive about the company's financial performance.

The stock market began to notice the positive effect that Asil Nadir had on company share prices, and market sentiment seemed to work in his favour. In July 1980 Polly Peck raised £1.5m in a rights issue, the new capital being required to purchase Uni-Pac, a company already owned by Nadir, which began packaging fruit in northern Cyprus. The Turkish Cypriot government, under its president Rauf Denktash, was keen to encourage inward investment into the economy, although there were no doubt concerns by investors about the status of the Turkish Cypriot economy and about potential difficulties in remitting cash from northern Cyprus.

Moving away from clothing, an industry which Nadir was experienced and familiar with, and diversifying into fruit packaging represented a risk. Polly Peck then acquired another small listed company, Cornell Dresses. Shortly after acquiring control, the share price of Cornell Dresses increased by approximately 400 per cent, which seems to have been related once again to positive market sentiment connected with Asil Nadir's business reputation.

Nadir then turned his attention to the Turkish mainland. He decided to set up a water-bottling plant at Niksar in 1982 and was expecting to sell bottled mineral water to Middle Eastern countries, a potentially lucrative market. In 1983 Nadir picked up another company in Turkey, involved in fruit packing and processing. That same year, he entered into a joint venture (Vestel) with the UK firm Thorn-EMI. Vestel would manufacture televisions and video-cassette recorders and was to prove a particularly profitable part of the Polly Peck group. Although many of Polly Peck's business ventures were ultimately profitable, some of them took time to come on stream, yet the stock market always seemed to have particularly optimistic expectations about the future profitability of these deals – perhaps unrealistically high expectations.

In the early 1980s, some financial journalists began to question the quality of information in Polly Peck's financial statements about current operations. Hindle refers to articles in *The Observer* in 1983 on the slow progress of the water-bottling plant at Niksar, and about the profit projections for the Thorn-EMI electronics venture. Michael Gillard, an *Observer* journalist, had questioned whether Polly Peck's UK auditors, Stoy Hayward, were carrying out proper checks on the Cypriot accounts, which were being audited by a local Cypriot firm.

> And why was there no geographical breakdown of profit and turnover in the accounts? The London Stock Exchange's rules demanded that quoted companies give such a breakdown, but Polly Peck had obtained a special exemption from the Stock Exchange on the grounds that giving such information would be 'commercially damaging'. This vacuum, said the *Observer*, 'only serves to encourage speculation, if not suspicion'. Mr Nadir did not help his case by refusing to meet Mr Gillard and put across his point of view. (Hindle, 1993: 52)

However, such negative comments seemed to have little impact on the share performance of Asil Nadir's companies. One explanation that has been offered is that the 1980s witnessed an era of increasing entrepreneurship engendered by the values of the Conservative government under Prime Minister Margaret Thatcher, who came to power in 1979. Also, Asil Nadir seemed to find little difficulty in raising the necessary finance for his projects from UK banks.

It is quite likely that the Conservative privatizations of the early 1980s influenced market sentiment. The privatizations of state-owned enterprises such as British Telecommunications had created a wider spread of share ownership, which gave an almost assured capital gain to those who subscribed for the shares. In this environment, Polly Peck was perhaps seen by many investors as a stock that could be relied on to produce above-normal profits well into the future.

During the 1980s it was also perceived by some observers that Polly Peck's operations in Cyprus might be at risk from political uncertainties. Asil Nadir had been able to negotiate some privileges for his companies' operations in northern Cyprus with the Turkish Cypriot president Rauf Denktash but there was always a danger that reunification of the island could end these favourable conditions.

But in the first half of the 1980s it appeared that some of Polly Peck's projects– the water-bottling plant in Turkey and the Vestel electronics plant – were taking longer to deliver revenues than had been anticipated.

Nevertheless, Polly Peck had a tendency to continually announce new and exciting ventures and this seemed to support investors' confidence in the shares and hence the share price.

POLLY PECK EXPANDS ABROAD

By 1985, Cornell Dresses and Wearwell had been incorporated in the Polly Peck Group, whose name was changed to Polly Peck International. Headquarters were established in Berkeley Square, an exclusive part of Mayfair in London. By 1986 Polly Peck shares could be traded in the USA and positive market sentiment there appears to have been partly responsible for a substantial rise in the Polly Peck share price in 1987.

Towards the end of 1987 Polly Peck was raising loan finance in Swiss francs for investment in countries such as Turkey. This did not appear to be a sound policy, raising finance in a stable currency to invest in a weak currency area. One of the problems with trying to interpret Polly Peck's financial position was the fact that a large part of its revenue was received in Turkey and northern Cyprus, where the local currency was the Turkish lira.

During 1988 Polly Peck began to buy companies or establish joint ventures in various countries, including the Netherlands, Spain, Hong Kong and the United States. In addition, Polly Peck was buying stakes in UK companies such as Borthwicks, involved in food processing. Polly Peck had also invested in shipping and by 1988 operated 10 ships with cargo and refrigeration facilities. As a result of organic growth combined with company takeovers, the group virtually doubled in size between 1987 and 1988. There was a danger that Polly Peck was over-reaching itself and would not be able to properly control so many diverse operations.

Even though he was both chairman and chief executive of Polly Peck International, Asil Nadir could not always persuade his board to agree to his corporate purchases and, instead, bought some operations (such as newspaper publishers in Turkey) from his own private resources.

In 1989, Del Monte – which processed tinned fruit and sold fresh fruit – came on to the market. The previous year, RJR Nabisco had been the subject of a leveraged buy-out, which had left the company with a substantial amount of debt to service. RJR Nabisco decided to sell Del Monte to reduce its debt. Polly Peck decided to bid for the fresh fruit business and paid $875m. As a result of this deal, Polly Peck's share price increased by over 20 per cent. This increase in market capitalization helped to push Polly Peck into the FTSE 100 index. The purchase of Del Monte was paid for partly through a rights issue and partly through debt, the major part being debt. In addition, the Del Monte brand was included on the Polly Peck balance sheet.

In 1989 Polly Peck acquired a 51 per cent stake in Sansui, a Japanese electronics company quoted on the Tokyo Stock Exchange. This purchase also increased Polly Peck's debt. In order to reduce debt, Polly Peck began to sell some operations that had formed the core of its business, and attempted to get Del Monte a quote on the New York Stock Exchange (NYSE), but was not successful. This would have raised additional equity for the Polly Peck group of companies and helped to reduce its overall level of debt.

NADIR TRIES TO TAKE POLLY PECK PRIVATE

In August 1990, an indication of Asil Nadir's management style came in an announcement that he would bid for Polly Peck International with the aim of converting it into a private group. On Friday 10 August 1990, Asil Nadir summoned the board of directors of Polly Peck to an extraordinary meeting two days later. After five hours of boardroom discussion, Polly Peck's finance director, David Fawcus, announced the possibility of a bid by Asil Nadir to take the group private. It appeared that Nadir was becoming frustrated by his conviction that the group's shares were 'undervalued' in the stock market.

For a long time Asil Nadir had felt that the group's price–earnings ratio was too low. The price–earnings ratio expresses the relationship between a company's share price and its earnings (essentially, reported profits before payment of dividends). Companies which operate in a relatively 'safe' economic environment tend to have higher price–earnings ratios compared to companies whose earnings are more volatile and perhaps seen as 'risky'. In August 1990, the price–earnings ratio of Polly Peck was about 8. Because a large part of Polly Peck's revenues were generated in northern Cyprus, whose international status was unclear, it was likely that the stock market would mark down the shares to some extent. But in 1990 there was an additional element of risk. On 2 August 1990, Iraqi armed forces invaded Kuwait, bringing instability to the Middle East – and much of Polly Peck's revenue was generated in Turkey, which shared a border with Iraq.

A report, shortly after Asil Nadir announced that he wanted to take Polly Peck private, stated:

> The precise fashion in which the group achieved its extraordinary profitability has never been fully apparent – then or now. In the City doubts began to circulate, fanned, most Turks believe, by Mr Nadir's enemies among the Greek Cypriots who were not unnaturally resentful of his success in making profits out of their former orange groves. Rumours that the Turkish Cypriot authorities were about to withdraw tax concessions helped fuel a market panic and a plunge in the share price. Distrust of Mr Nadir was exacerbated by a campaign against him by some British papers. (*Financial Times,* 14 August 1990: 15)

At first, commentators appeared to be generally sympathetic to Asil Nadir's move to take Polly Peck private. While Turkey and northern Cyprus were important to Polly Peck's operations, together revenues generated in the Eastern Mediterranean comprised only about 30 per cent of the group total. Nadir's frustration with what he viewed as a low stock-market valuation seemed to be a reasonable justification for him to want to take the group private. However, five days after announcing his intention to take the group private, Asil Nadir abruptly changed his mind, and announced that he was dropping the plan. This abrupt change on Nadir's part did not go down well in the market. The share price fell substantially over the course of one week. Before the announcement, the share price stood at 393p, equivalent to a market capitalization of £1.9bn. After Asil Nadir announced that he would not take the group private, the share price fell to 307p, equivalent to a market capitalization of £1.3bn. In the course of a week, approximately £600m had been wiped off the equity value of the group. This event seemed to be a turning point in Polly Peck's fortunes.

THE STOCK EXCHANGE INVESTIGATES

Nadir alleged that he had dropped his plans to take the company private after receiving approaches from 'significant institutional and private shareholders' who wanted Polly Peck to remain public.[1] The London Stock Exchange was keen to investigate quickly the circumstances surrounding the two announcements by Asil Nadir, particularly in view of the fluctuations in the share price. He had claimed that there was no doubt as to the availability of finance to make an offer for the company. His private shareholdings in Polly Peck amounted to 26 per cent and he would need acceptances from other shareholders of 64 per cent to arrive at the critical level of 90 per cent of the group's shares. A statement[2] issued by the Stock Exchange, following the investigation, noted a lack of preparation to normal standards by Mr Nadir before he notified the board of his intention to make an offer for Polly Peck. It also referred to the fact that Mr Nadir convened an emergency board meeting for Sunday 12 August 1990 at very short notice and this contributed to the fact that only seven of the thirteen directors were able to attend. Also, given the short notice, the board did not have access to adequate professional advice on a suitable response to Mr Nadir's approach. Somewhat ominously, the Stock Exchange reported that it had conveyed its findings and the supporting papers to the relevant authorities. There is little doubt that a main concern of the Stock Exchange was that anyone with privileged information on the announcements could have exploited the opportunity to benefit financially from the share price fluctuations.

But, by early September 1990, Polly Peck appeared to have put the August controversy behind it and announced on 3 September 1990 financial results for the first half of the financial year: they were better than market forecasts had suggested. Polly Peck also announced a 21 per cent increase in its interim dividend, but at a meeting with analysts, in answer to a question, Asil Nadir was forced to issue a categorical denial that he was under investigation.[3] Then on 20 September 1990, Asil Nadir was interviewed by the Serious Fraud Office (SFO) and questioned for several hours. On 19 September the Metropolitan Police had searched the offices of South Audley Management, a property company indirectly linked to Nadir. It appeared that South Audley Management and a former director had been investigated by the Stock Exchange insider dealing group.

It was also reported that the Turkish Government had made representations to the UK Prime Minister concerning what it believed to be a campaign against Nadir, manipulated by Greek Cypriots. On Thursday 20 September 1990, the share price of Polly Peck had collapsed and trading was suspended at a price of 108p. The falling share price coincided with Asil Nadir's questioning by the Serious Fraud Office. The fall in share price left Polly Peck with a market capitalization of £468m, about a quarter of what it had been two months earlier.

On 23 September 1990 the *Sunday Times* published a lengthy article which alleged that there had been irregularities in share dealings in Polly Peck shares. The article cited Jason Davies, a broker based in Switzerland who worked for Asil Nadir's private companies. The article went on to explain:

> For some weeks, well before the SFO entered the scene, the *Sunday Times* Insight team had been investigating Nadir, Davies and their associates. It has uncovered how: for months Davies and others ran a share-buying operation to bolster the fortune and reputation of both Nadir and Polly Peck; a complex network of letter-box companies and foreign bank accounts was used to disguise the scheme and hide it from the prying eyes of City regulators. (*Sunday Times*, 23 September 1990, Business Section)

The *Sunday Times* article also referred to an incident in May 1989. David Fawcus, finance director of Polly Peck, and Tony Reading, managing director, were surprised to learn that a number of key staff had suddenly been dismissed by Asil Nadir. The dismissed staff included Martin Helme, finance director of Sunzest (a Polly Peck subsidiary); Vi Jensen, financial controller; Martin Brown, another Sunzest executive; and even David Fawcus's own secretary. When the news reached the stock market, Polly Peck's shares dropped by 10 per cent amid fears that Tony Reading might resign. In the event Tony Reading did resign a month later, although David Fawcus stayed on and did not resign until early 1991, by which time administrators had been appointed to manage Polly Peck.

The *Sunday Times* article of 23 September 1990 raised the possibility that Polly Peck money might have been used to buy Polly Peck shares. 'If they did so, it would send misleading signals to the market. Pension funds and trusts, which look after the savings of millions of ordinary people, as well as private investors and speculators, rely on share prices to guide their investment decisions. They assume that price reflects thousands of independent decisions to buy, hold or sell. Financial assistance by a company for the acquisition of its own shares is therefore outlawed'.[4]

By Monday 24 September 1990, it was being reported[5] that some financial institutions were calling for the appointment of an independent chairman. There were also requests that independent reporting accountants be brought in alongside Polly Peck's established auditors, Stoy Hayward. On Wednesday 26 September 1990, it was revealed[6] that the Takeover Panel had uncovered trades in shares of Polly Peck International worth nearly £2m, which were undisclosed for six weeks in breach of the Takeover Code. It was reported that sales of Polly Peck shares at 417p and 410p were made near the top of the market following Asil Nadir's announcement to buy out the company. It was also stated that rule 8.3 of the Takeover Code requires all deals by any shareholder controlling more than 1 per cent of any company to be disclosed by noon the day after they were carried out, once a formal bid period has begun. The shares in question had been sold two days after the Polly Peck board announced the approach by Asil Nadir to buy out the remaining Polly Peck shares.

POLLY PECK'S LIQUIDITY PROBLEMS

On Monday 1 October 1990, Polly Peck International delivered a statement[7] on the crisis which had overtaken the company since Asil Nadir had proposed to buy out the remaining Polly Peck shareholders on 12 August 1990. It stated that the share price collapse and associated negative publicity had precipitated liquidity problems for the parent company. The board emphasized that these liquidity problems related to the parent company rather than to operating subsidiaries which they claimed had a very successful trading record. The board went on to say that one of its most urgent tasks was to see a restoration of confidence in the company. In addition Mr Nadir had informed the board that he denied all allegations of impropriety and he had commenced proceedings for libel against the *Sunday Times* and *Observer* newspapers.

In early October 1990 *The Guardian* reported that Asil Nadir was jetting around the world struggling to save his corporate empire and that the financial chaos surrounding Polly Peck threatened to spread to other companies built up and dominated by charismatic individuals. In an interesting article,[8] Roger Cowe referred also to Rupert Murdoch and Robert Maxwell as striving to avoid joining the list of debt-bound businesses whose extraordinary growth during the 1980s was in danger of being followed by dramatic collapse in the 1990s. This was a particularly insightful comment given that the Maxwell empire collapsed just over a year later under a mountain of debt. Cowe was particularly concerned about independent scrutiny of chairmen who dominated their boards of directors in quoted companies. 'Look in vain for strong directors, executive or non-executive, who can stand up to the charismatic boss, not merely to verify transactions with private interests, but also to challenge their whims'.[9]

The reason for the collapse in the share price became clearer some two weeks later. It was reported[10] that banks who were holding Polly Peck shares, as collateral against loans advanced to Asil Nadir, dumped 10m shares on the market on 20 September 1990 and this precipitated a collapse in the company's share price. Once the share price fell, the shares Nadir had pledged as collateral would be insufficient and he would need to increase the collateral. On 21 September 1990 the Zurich office of Warburg's sold a further 2.6m shares. In total over 16m shares were sold by financial institutions before the share price suspension, the largest single sale being 7.9m shares sold by Citicorp investment bank on 20 September 1990.

On 3 October 1990, Polly Peck announced that it had halted payments to creditors. An adviser to Asil Nadir claimed[11] that Polly Peck's liquidity problems had arisen because the Sheraton Voyager Hotel, which had been built in the Turkish coastal resort of Antalya at a cost of £70m, had been financed not by an increase in debt but out of the group's cash flow. A meeting with its banks was scheduled for 5 October and there was some expectation that Turkish financial institutions would be willing to provide financial assistance to Polly Peck during its liquidity crisis. It was learned that Polly Peck was facing difficulties remitting cash from northern Cyprus.

On 4 October 1990 Asil Nadir appeared to be confident about his financial position and claimed that his personal wealth was eight to ten times the value of his 24 per cent holding in Polly Peck. However, it was not known to what extent this holding was pledged against bank loans. At the suspension price, this made his personal wealth worth about £1bn. He claimed that he had substantial assets in Turkey and northern Cyprus. By 8 October it seemed unlikely that the Turkish President, Turgut Ozal, would be willing to mount a rescue operation for Polly Peck, but Nadir hoped to gain a standstill on interest payments and a rollover of short-term debt. He stated that he was negotiating to dispose of assets and reduce the company's gearing.

On 10 October 1990, Asil Nadir flew to Turkey to begin negotiations with government officials, banks and businesses in order to try to resolve Polly Peck's financial crisis. Speaking from Turkey on 11 October, Nadir claimed that he would be able to offer 'serious evidence of good amounts of remittances from Turkey and Cyprus'.[12] He needed to provide solid evidence to the creditors of Polly Peck that he could produce cash to persuade the banks to roll over the existing loans. Asil Nadir was desperate to dispose of assets in Turkey and northern Cyprus, but appeared to be facing difficulties in getting potential purchasers interested in bidding for Polly Peck's businesses in the eastern Mediterranean.

By 23 October, one banker in Istanbul was quoted as saying 'Mr Nadir is not succeeding in selling anything here, including his personal assets, and he has no way out now'.[13] Already, Polly Peck had made more than 100 employees redundant in Cyprus and it was feared that there would be further job losses, given that Polly Peck was the largest employer in northern Cyprus with 8,000 employees.

THE COURT APPOINTS ADMINISTRATORS

Polly Peck was placed into administration on 25 October 1990 after the company was unable to satisfy its bankers that it would be able to reduce its debts. In addition, Asil Nadir himself faced personal bankruptcy when Barclays de Zoete Wedd attempted to serve a personal bankruptcy petition against him for £3.6m unpaid debt relating to Polly Peck shares purchased the previous month.

> The descent from being one of the UK's thirty-six wealthiest individuals to defendant in a bankruptcy action had occurred over just a few weeks, and could have easily been avoided. It was the result of his repeated purchases of Polly Peck shares during the autumn as the share price tumbled. Taken all together, his last-ditch purchases totalled between £40 million and £50 million, and on top of this were liabilities to the Inland Revenue believed to be about £20 million. If it seems remarkable that Asil Nadir would have made purchases on this scale while his empire was tottering around him, it may seem even more astonishing that the securities houses with whom he traded allowed themselves to become involved in risky transactions on this scale when a moment's reflection would have warned them of what might lie ahead. (Barchard, 1992: 247)

On 30 October the Serious Fraud Office (SFO) arranged for police and accountants to search the London headquarters of Polly Peck and it was reported that debts owing to creditors exceeded £1.3bn. Matters went from bad to worse when, on 17 December 1990, Asil Nadir was charged with 18 offences of theft and false accounting. He had been arrested on 15 December at Heathrow Airport, London, when he had returned from a month's visit to Turkey and northern Cyprus in an attempt to dispose of assets and raise cash.

There appeared to be differences between administrators and the SFO. The administrators had reportedly warned that Nadir's arrest might hinder their work. They had previously complained of disruption when the SFO searched Polly Peck's London headquarters at Berkeley Square on 30 October and removed papers from the building.

After Nadir's arrest on 15 December 1990, bail was set at £3.5m and Nadir was forced to spend several days in Brixton jail while the bail conditions were met. In addition, Nadir had to surrender his passports. The bail conditions appeared to some observers to be quite severe. In November 1991, Asil Nadir had been made personally bankrupt which meant that he had to give up his UK company directorships, including chairman and chief executive of Polly Peck. In February 1992, Nadir was committed for trial at the Old Bailey.

At first the administrators[14] had decided to co-operate with Asil Nadir, since they believed that the shareholders and creditors would ultimately receive more through co-operation than through legal action, but in October 1991 the administrators sued him for damages. In May 1991 the administrators had predicted that the shareholders and creditors would receive 52 pence for every £1 they had lost. By 1993, it seemed that the creditors would receive only 4 pence in the pound. By June 1991 the administrators' costs amounted to £8.4m.

> At the end of the day administrators are judged by what they can retrieve for creditors and shareholders. If in Polly Peck's case this turns out to be less than they earn in fees for themselves it will not be the first time in British corporate history that the process of administration has been a complete fiasco. (Hindle, 1993: 224)

ASIL NADIR FLEES TO CYPRUS

In May 1993, Asil Nadir decided to break his bail conditions and escape to northern Cyprus. Shortly after his escape to Cyprus, *The Independent* speculated that Asil Nadir had decided to 'jump bail' because four applications for a relaxation of his bail conditions had already been rejected by the UK courts. In addition he may have suspected that he would be charged with conspiring to pervert the course of justice (by withholding information), which could mean that his bail would be revoked.[15] Apart from the criminal prosecution, Nadir was being sued for £378m in the civil courts by the Polly Peck administrators, and creditors were claiming a further £80m from him.

Nadir has effectively been in exile in northern Cyprus since May 1993 and, given the particular international legal status of northern Cyprus, has managed to avoid extradition to face the courts in the UK. Although in 2003 Nadir suggested that he wanted to return to the UK to face the courts and clear his name, the SFO stated that he still faced 66 counts of theft. From Nadir's point of view he would probably face arrest as soon as he set foot in the UK. At the time of writing, unless Nadir does decide to return voluntarily to the UK, his trial is likely to resume only if northern Cyprus becomes part of the European Union. Until that time and the resumption of the court proceedings, many questions related to this case are unlikely to be resolved.

DISCUSSION

Could, or should, the events which overtook Polly Peck in 1990 have been foreseen? With hindsight it is possible to argue that the stock market was fixated on the remarkable share price performance of Polly Peck during the 1980s. Stock market sentiment may have been placing unreasonable expectations on the future profits that Polly Peck would be able to deliver. Although some were critical of the basis for Polly Peck's share price movements, critics – especially during Polly Peck's heyday – seemed to be in a small minority. Barchard (1992: 255) refers to one Swiss shareholder in Polly Peck who recalled being laughed down by other investors when he questioned the treatment of foreign exchange losses at an annual general meeting.

Gwilliam and Russell believe that financial analysts were insufficiently critical of Polly Peck's financial statements and argue (1991: 25) that 'a significant proportion of analysts either did not dig sufficiently deep into the disclosed information or failed to understand its importance'. They comment on the fact that Polly Peck held monetary assets in Turkey and northern Cyprus in a depreciating currency, the Turkish lira. In this situation, holdings in the local currency would be subject to exchange losses over time as the Turkish lira depreciated against the pound sterling. However, a depreciating currency, by its very nature, will also be associated with high levels of interest on deposits (as compensation for the depreciating currency).

Gwilliam and Russell also refer to the fact that in 1989 Polly Peck's interest received was greater than interest payable, a surprising result since at the beginning and end of the financial year monetary liabilities exceeded monetary assets. The relevant UK accounting standard, SSAP 20, *Foreign Currency Translation* (ASB) allowed foreign exchange losses to be taken to reserves, rather than be deducted from profit in the profit-and-loss account. But a case could be made for charging foreign exchange losses directly to the profit-and-loss account. Nevertheless, full information was provided in Polly Peck's accounts through the notes. As Gwilliam and Russell (1991: 25) state, 'Polly Peck's accounts were full of danger signs. So why did the analysts still say "buy"?'

The fact that Asil Nadir was both chairman and chief executive of Polly Peck was also a cause for concern. The concentration of too much power in the hands of one individual may have meant that important decisions were not fully discussed by the board of directors. Hindle (1993: 153) states that in 1990:

> The reality was that Mr Nadir was juggling with so many balls at the time that he did not have the capacity to watch them all with his usual intensity. Superior information and a hands-on will to succeed had always been at the heart of his commercial successes. Now he was sometimes not getting the information, or not absorbing what he was getting.

In February 1991, an auction of furnishings at the London headquarters of Polly Peck, in Berkeley Square, raised about £3m. It was reported that Nadir had invested heavily in 18th-century English furniture and had spent about £7m on the Polly Peck corporate collection.[16] It has to be wondered whether such expenditures were of benefit to Polly Peck. Could they have been used more profitably elsewhere in the group?

Finally concerns have been expressed in the media[17] about the legal process following Asil Nadir's arrest in December 1990 and the length of time it took for the UK authorities to bring the case to trial. Initially, Nadir was charged with 59 counts of theft and false accounting, but in 1992 a judge threw out 46 charges, leaving 13 charges relating to £31m. When Nadir fled in May 1993, two and a half years after Polly Peck collapsed, the trial had not yet started and Nadir was under quite restrictive bail conditions. It is perhaps not surprising that he became impatient with the delays in the legal process. What is clear is that until the legal process can resume, there will be no definitive answer to many of the issues surrounding this complex affair.

Table 5.1 *Polly Peck: key events*

1941	Asil Nadir born in Cyprus
1959	Nadir family emigrates to London
1973	Wearwell is floated on London Stock Exchange
1980	Nadir gains control of Polly Peck
1982	Niksar water-bottling plant set up in Turkey
1983	Vestel joint venture (with Thorn-EMI)
1985	Company name changed to Polly Peck International and headquarters moved to Berkeley Square, London
1989	Polly Peck buys Del Monte and 51% stake in Sansui
1990	Nadir announces private bid for Polly Peck (August); Nadir interviewed by SFO (September); Polly Peck placed in administration (October); Nadir arrested (December)
1993	Asil Nadir flees to northern Cyprus

Discussion questions

1 Discuss the advantages and disadvantages of allowing one individual to act as both chairman and chief executive of a quoted company.
2 Should the banks have been more cautious in lending to Polly Peck and to Asil Nadir?
3 What do you believe are the main lessons that can be drawn from the collapse of Polly Peck?
4 Identify the stakeholders who were most disadvantaged by the collapse of Polly Peck.
5 Discuss the proposition that it is not in a quoted company's best interests for the directors to own a substantial proportion of the share capital.

REFERENCES

Accounting Standards Board, *SSAP 20: Foreign Currency Translation*. London: ASB.

Barchard, D. (1992) *Asil Nadir: The Rise and Fall of Polly Peck*. London: Victor Gollancz.

Gwilliam, D. and Russell, T. (1991) 'Polly Peck: where were the analysts?', *Accountancy*, January: 25–6.

Hindle, T. (1993) *Asil Nadir: Fugitive from Injustice?* London: Pan Books.

Smith, T. (1996) *Accounting for Growth*, 2nd edn. London: Century Business.

NOTES

1 *Financial Times*, 21 August 1990: 17.

2 See *Financial Times*, 25 August 1990: 8.

3 *Financial Times*, 4 September 1990: 21.

4 *Sunday Times*, 23 September 1990, Business Section.

5 *Independent*, 25 September 1990: 22.

6 *Financial Times*, 27 September 1990: 24.

7 *Financial Times*, 2 October 1990: 27.

8 *Guardian*, 2 October 1990.

9 *Guardian*, 2 October 1990.

10 *Financial Times*, 2 October 1990: 27.

11 *Financial Times*, 4 October 1990: 1.

12 *Financial Times*, 12 October 1990: 1.

13 *Financial Times*, 24 October 1990: 19.

14 In October 1992 two of the administrators, Michael Jordan and Richard Stone, were fined £1,000 by the Institute of Chartered Accountants in England and Wales on the grounds that their company, Cork Gully, was a subsidiary of Coopers and Lybrand, which had carried out consultancy work for Polly Peck.

15 *Independent*, 9 May 1993: 17.

16 *Financial Times*, 20 February 1991: 20.

17 See *Independent*, 9 May 1993: 17.

Bank of Credit and Commerce International (BCCI)

SIX

In the summer of 1991, Bank of Credit and Commerce International (BCCI) was by all accounts only weeks away from financial collapse. Systematic fraud, over a number of years and reaching up to the senior management, finally meant that the bank would be unable to continue operating. Bank regulators in a number of countries decided to act before that happened. Although they had suspected for some time that there were irregularities in the bank's activities, they had decided to wait until they could co-ordinate their actions and try to bring about an orderly run-down of BCCI's operations.

In the UK, BCCI had 25 branches and, on Friday 5 July 1991, Bank of England officials closed all the branches and employees were ordered to leave. At the same time, regulators in other countries – including the United States, France, the Cayman Islands, Spain and Switzerland – moved on BCCI's branches and offices. In addition, 60 countries had been warned of the action by the regulators and asked to co-operate. Pakistan was one of the few countries that did not close down BCCI's branches. Another was Abu Dhabi, where branches of BCCI were allowed to continue operating and news of the closures in Europe and the USA was censored. But, by Sunday 7 July 1991, BCCI's offices in 18 countries had been closed and its operations restricted in 40 other countries.

The Governor of the Bank of England, Robin Leigh-Pemberton, was quoted as saying that fraud had been perpetrated at the highest levels within BCCI.[1] BCCI was a large international bank, with branches in over 70 countries around the world. Planning the closure was a complex task and necessitated close co-operation by banking authorities in different countries. It was most important that the regulators' move to shut down BCCI should be kept secret to avoid any possible danger of creating instability in the financial markets.

Soon after the Bank of England stepped in to close down BCCI branches in the UK, considerable criticism was levelled at the Bank of England, which was seen as being responsible for thousands of individuals losing their savings. The Bank of England's response was that, if it had warned investors to remove their savings before it took action, this would have resulted in a disastrous run on the bank (BCCI). No doubt the Bank of England believed that a few lucky depositors would have been able to retrieve all their savings, leaving a large number of unfortunate depositors with little or nothing. So it was preferable, according to the Bank of England, to try to bring about an orderly shutdown of BCCI's operations in order that something might be salvaged for all the depositors.

The founder of BCCI, Agha Hasan Abedi, registered the parent company of the group, BCCI Holdings SA, in Luxembourg. A major subsidiary, BCCI Overseas, was registered in the Cayman Islands. Adams and Frantz state that:

> There is some lingering uncertainty about why Abedi split his operation into its Luxembourg and Cayman Islands halves, but he seemed perfectly happy with the result – that no central regulator knew what was happening inside the bank. He certainly chose host countries where the regulators were notoriously lax, and BCCI's financial picture was muddy to begin with. The regulatory arrangement and the secrecy surrounding the Middle Eastern shareholders made it impossible to get a consolidated assessment of the bank's finances. (Adams and Frantz, 1993: 46)

Shortly after BCCI was closed down, the UK Prime Minister, John Major, commissioned Lord Justice Bingham to report on events at BCCI. When the report was published in 1992, Bingham did not recommend a radical shake-up of banking supervision in the UK. Instead, some suggestions were made to improve the existing system of banking supervision. Bingham noted that the most important single lesson was that banking group structures that were deliberately made complex in order to deny supervisors a clear view of a bank's operations should be outlawed. In addition, Bingham suggested there should be improved exchange of information between international supervisors and a tougher line should be taken against financial centres that offered impenetrable secrecy.

The official line (the Bingham Report) attached a major share of the blame to the Bank of England. The auditors, Price Waterhouse, received relatively little criticism, but much of it questioned whether Price Waterhouse had been sufficiently blunt in their warnings to the Bank of England.

AGHA HASAN ABEDI

BCCI had been founded in 1972 by Agha Hasan Abedi, who began his business career by working for Habib Bank in Karachi, Pakistan, in the 1950s. He appears to have progressed well in the bank and received a number of promotions. According to one account,[2] Abedi was keen to expand banking into areas that would benefit the poorer section of society and less developed countries in particular. By the mid-1960s Abedi was working for United Bank, based in Pakistan, and in 1966 he had an important meeting with Sheikh Zayed bin Sultan al-Nahayan of Abu Dhabi. Zayed had just established himself as the ruler of the small Middle Eastern Gulf state. Abedi successfully negotiated the opening of a branch of United Bank in Abu Dhabi, as well as the right to act as banker for Pakistani workers there. The fact that Abedi was himself a Shiite Muslim assisted his business dealings in the Middle East. Sheikh Zayed was to prove to be a powerful and influential backer of BCCI, along with a number of other shareholders in Abu Dhabi and the Middle East.

In 1972 President Zulfikar Ali Bhutto announced a programme to nationalize Pakistani-based banks. A number of important bankers, including Abedi, were placed under house arrest and it was at this time that Abedi planned a new bank, Bank of Credit and Commerce International (BCCI). Abedi was successful in securing the backing of Sheikh Zayed for his new venture, which allowed Abedi to resign from United Bank and set up BCCI with offices in Abu Dhabi and Pakistan. One of Abedi's early associates in the venture was Swaleh Naqvi, who was to take over from Abedi in 1988.

POLITICAL INFLUENCE

Abedi made considerable efforts to attract important political figures to back his bank. One of these was Jimmy Carter, president of the United States from 1977 to 1981. Carter assisted Abedi in developing links in China and other developing countries. Another important political figure was Clark Clifford, a well-known and highly respected adviser to the Democratic Party in the USA, going back to President Truman in the 1940s and President Kennedy in the 1960s.

In 1998, Clark Clifford and his law partner Robert Altman reached a $5m settlement with the US Federal Reserve Board related to court charges subsequent to the BCCI collapse in 1991. A group of Arab investors had succeeded in taking over a US bank, First American Bankshares, and Clifford was appointed as chairman. He had reassured the Federal Reserve Board that BCCI would not control First American Bankshares. However, it later turned out that the parent company of First American Bankshares was in fact controlled by BCCI. There is little doubt that, without Clifford's status and respectability, the US Federal Reserve Board would not have allowed the takeover. To make matters worse, it was also revealed that Clifford had made a profit of some $6m from holding bank shares bought with an unsecured loan from BCCI.[3]

Lord Callaghan (who had been UK Prime Minister from 1976 to 1979) was reported as saying in the House of Lords 'The people whom I know in the bank [BCCI] are men of propriety and integrity'.[4] In fact Callaghan had at one time tried to persuade Robin Leigh-Pemberton, Governor of the Bank of England, to bring BCCI to England, but the headquarters of BCCI had remained in Luxembourg where banking regulations were less stringent.[5]

For Abedi himself these connections were to prove to be extremely useful when, in 1988, he suffered a severe heart attack at his home in London. The former US president Jimmy Carter personally telephoned an eminent surgeon, Dr Norman Shumway, and persuaded him to fly to London to assist with a heart transplant operation.[6]

BCCI'S INITIAL PROBLEMS

It seems that the start of BCCI's troubles can be traced to financial problems with one of its major customers, Gulf Group, a shipping company. In the 1970s Gulf Group began to get into difficulties and was unable to repay its loans. Abedi and Naqvi became concerned that if the extent of the non-performing loans became known, then bank regulators would close BCCI. The evidence suggests that Abedi and Naqvi took the decision to falsify BCCI's accounts in order to hide the losses and allow the reported reserves to appear healthy.

BCCI was in a particularly vulnerable position because, as an international bank, it had no official lender of last resort. So any rescue of BCCI in the event of financial collapse would depend on the goodwill of the Abu Dhabi shareholders in injecting more equity. As it turned out, this is what happened and the Abu Dhabi shareholders did in fact provide additional equity. What will never be known for certain is whether the reorganization and refinancing plan that Price Waterhouse was trying to promote in June 1991, just before the shutdown, would have been successful in saving BCCI.

From 1978 BCCI operated the Gulf Group accounts as if the company was a going concern. BCCI had to deceive the regulators into believing that Gulf Group could meet its interest payments and principal repayments. BCCI even went so far as to settle Gulf Group's debts with its creditors. But in order to keep up this pretence, BCCI needed an inflow of cash to meet the cash payments. This was achieved by securing additional deposits from customers who were attracted by higher rates of interest. BCCI was effectively operating a 'Ponzi scheme', named after Charles Ponzi, an Italian immigrant living in Boston, USA, in 1919. Ponzi attracted investors by offering huge investment returns. However, capital invested by new investors was simply used to pay a return to established investors. Inevitably the original Ponzi scheme collapsed and it was estimated that 20,000 investors lost in total $20m.[7]

During the 1980s BCCI became heavily involved in laundering money illegally earned by drug dealers in Colombia. Manuel Noriega, a Panamanian general who had been an important client of BCCI, eventually faced trial in the USA. As an international bank, BCCI was well placed to facilitate the clandestine transfer of large sums of cash around the world.

In October 1988 US police and customs officers, following a lengthy undercover operation, arrested seven BCCI officials in Tampa, Florida, on drug-trafficking and money-laundering charges. Eleven BCCI officials were named in an indictment by a federal grand jury in Tampa. It would seem that the Tampa trial, which was widely reported at the time, should have served as a clear warning to the Bank of England of problems with BCCI's operations.

BCCI'S AUDITORS

The audit of BCCI was initially shared between two firms, Ernst and Whinney, and Price Waterhouse. However, in 1987, after substantial financial losses were discovered, Abedi agreed to the appointment of sole auditors and Price Waterhouse accepted the appointment. In 1988 Price Waterhouse gave a qualified audit, which related to uncertainty over the impact of the criminal charges brought against BCCI officials in the United States. In 1989 a senior employee with BCCI alerted Price Waterhouse to the possibility of fraud. For instance, the authenticity of some loans was in doubt as well as information given by BCCI management to the auditors.

As a result of these allegations, Price Waterhouse requested a meeting with the Bank of England. At the meeting in February 1990, Roger Barnes (for the Bank of England) was informed of the Price Waterhouse concerns by two partners, Tim Hoult and Chris Cowan. In 1992, Lord Bingham stated:

> I find it surprising that this meeting made so little impression on Barnes ... After years of criticism, and after Tampa, here was a suggestion of dishonesty from an unimpeachable source pointing at the chief executive of the group. Barnes' impassivity on receiving this message seems to me to show a rooted unwillingness to believe ill of BCCI. (*Accountancy*, December 1992: 16)

Lord Bingham had also stated that 'A reputable auditor does not voice doubts about the probity of his client to a regulator unless he has something fairly substantial to go on'.[8]

Then, four weeks after that first meeting, Hoult and Cowan again met with Barnes to state that Swaleh Naqvi, the chief executive of BCCI, had admitted that false documentation had been prepared to deceive the auditors. Naqvi had recently been appointed chief executive following the retirement of Abedi on grounds of ill health and, in his own defence, Naqvi argued that he had inherited 'a bad bank'.[9] Hoult and Cowan could offer little in the way of concrete evidence of fraud to Barnes, but nevertheless the Bank of England might have been expected to take the allegations more seriously.

The discussions between Price Waterhouse and Naqvi led to the creation of a task force to investigate the concerns which had been raised. On 18 April 1990, Price Waterhouse reported that they had found further irregularities. BCCI would need $1.8bn in financial support to keep going. Naqvi had to appeal to the shareholders in Abu Dhabi for an injection of equity to rescue the bank and $400m in additional equity was raised. Price Waterhouse was in a difficult position. If it had qualified the accounts, then it was possible that the shareholders would refuse to provide additional funds and BCCI would collapse. On the other hand, Price Waterhouse was concerned that allowing BCCI to continue operating could be storing up even greater problems for the future. For Price Waterhouse there were two important issues. The first related to the financial viability of BCCI, which was a real concern to Price Waterhouse but had, even if temporarily, been addressed by the additional $400m equity. The other issue concerned the possibility of fraud, for which Price Waterhouse had less tangible evidence.

In November 1990, Price Waterhouse was able to access Naqvi's personal files and found evidence relating to the falsification of accounts, using nominees. Price Waterhouse then drew up a report, which estimated that between $4.4bn and $5.6bn would be needed to support BCCI. There followed a meeting with BCCI directors, at which the frauds and malpractices were outlined. This particular report was not passed to the Bank of England, the reason being that Price Waterhouse felt that much of the information had already been given to the Bank of England.

Price Waterhouse was now anxious to move ahead with the refinancing and restructuring of BCCI, which seemed likely to receive the support of the Abu Dhabi shareholders: they would be responsible for additional equity of up to $5.1bn. On 22 June 1991, Price Waterhouse gave a further report to the Bank of England which included details of the fraud at BCCI. Finally, the Bank of England decided to act. The latest report had come as a 'devastating surprise' to the Bank of England, but should not have done so 'if the Bank had been more alert in receiving and understanding the messages it was given'.[10] There was also some criticism of Price Waterhouse, although muted, when Bingham stated that 'The report would not have come to the Bank as such a surprise either if Price Waterhouse . . . had more plainly and directly, more consistently, more comprehensively, and if they felt their messages were not being received, more vigorously, brought them to the notice of the Bank'.[11]

The Bank of England decided on 28 June 1991 not to allow the restructuring but instead to shut down BCCI. Price Waterhouse were not informed until 3 July 1991, just two days before the closure. Price Waterhouse were strongly opposed to the closure since the firm believed that a rescue with the help of the Abu Dhabi shareholders was feasible. Nevertheless, the Bank of England went ahead with the closure.

THE BINGHAM REPORT

The Bingham Report was critical of Price Waterhouse, but the bulk of the criticism was directed at the Bank of England. A potential conflict of interest for Price Waterhouse was that the firm was acting as the auditor of BCCI, while at the same time consultancy sections of Price Waterhouse were advising on the financial reorganization of BCCI to overcome the financial losses from the fraud that had taken place. In the House of Commons, Diane Abbott MP questioned the fact that 'On the one hand, [Price Waterhouse] was supposed to be BCCI's auditor, while on the other hand, it was earning huge fees from other parts of BCCI as management consultants'.[12] Norman Lamont, as Chancellor of the Exchequer, defended Price Waterhouse, saying that a careful reading of the Bingham report showed that Price Waterhouse had passed its concerns to the Bank of England on several occasions.

Despite the concerns raised about the potential difficulties when two different auditing firms audit an international bank, Bingham did not believe that this should be made absolutely unacceptable. While there were advantages to having a single audit firm, he believed it would not be desirable to impose a uniform rule.

Lord Bingham recognised the vital role played by the employee who first drew the attention of Price Waterhouse to the fraud at BCCI and paid tribute to his courage. It seems likely that without the whistleblower's actions, Price Waterhouse would have taken longer to gather evidence of the fraud.

One account described the Bingham Report as marking 'the most devastating public criticism levelled at the Bank of England in its 298-year history'.[13] Although the Labour Opposition called for the resignation of the Governor of the Bank of England, Robin Leigh-Pemberton, he did not resign. In the United States, Senator John Kerry had accused the Bank of England in its supervisory role as being 'wholly inadequate'.[14]

Bingham's language was more restrained, but the criticism was nevertheless fundamental:

> [Bingham] identified what he called a 'problem of culture' at the Bank, where officials were 'rather easily deterred', shied away from tackling difficult problems head-on, were over-concerned about public criticism, and repeatedly made 'inadequate' responses on supervisory matters. They also appeared more interested in maintaining the dignity of their position, to the point where they assumed people would come to them. It seldom occurred to them to go out and visit, say, officials in Abu Dhabi, to investigate what was happening in the world outside their own building. (*Sunday Times*, 25 October 1992, Business Section)

In other words, the Bank of England was not seen to be sufficiently active in following up the concerns expressed. And Price Waterhouse was not the first to express such concerns. The Bingham Report revealed that, as far back as 1978, the Bank had reservations about trusting the founder, Agha Hasan Abedi. In June 1982 a Bank of England official had warned that BCCI's structure made it very difficult to regulate, that its Luxembourg location was a fiction and that the Bank of England should not rely on assurances by the Luxembourg authorities. In 1988 the Bank of England received information – from diplomatic sources and the City of London fraud squad – that there was evidence of fraud at BCCI. Despite all these indications and warnings, the Bank of England took little concrete action.

The Bingham report cites ineptitude and negligence by Bank officials on a widespread scale. The report says Bank officials did not understand their powers, or their responsibilities to intervene in BCCI's affairs under the 1979 Banking Act. Their consistent response for more than a decade to the growing complexity of BCCI's operations – and to a series of allegations that it was involved in fraud – was to shy away from supervising it more closely, for fear that the job was simply too big and complex (*Financial Times*, 24 October 1992: 7).

Bingham considered whether the Price Waterhouse report in June 1991 should have come as such a great shock to the Bank of England:

> In my opinion it certainly should not. It would not have done so if the Bank had been more alert in receiving and understanding the messages it was given, if those messages (received and understood) had been more consistently brought to the attention of the most senior echelons in the Bank and the Board of Banking supervision and if the Bank had more actively pursued the leads it was given. (*Independent*, 23 October 1992: 22)

AN ALTERNATIVE VIEW

In contrast to the 'official view', an alternative view is offered by Mitchell et al. (2001). Mitchell et al. argue that in the mid-1980s Ernst and Young were sufficiently concerned about the poor internal controls at BCCI that they declined to be re-appointed as auditors unless they were given responsibility for auditing the entire BCCI group and unless BCCI implemented major improvements (Mitchell et al., 2001: 32). The Bank of England agreed that a single auditor was preferable, but instead the audit was given to Price Waterhouse, although they were not able to gain satisfactory access to accounts in some countries.

A problem identified with the audit of BCCI was that the auditors had a conflict of interest between their duty to make appropriate disclosures to the bank regulators and their need to retain the confidence of their client. Although it might be thought that Price Waterhouse was a global firm, in fact its national branches operate with a considerable degree of autonomy from each other. A report to the US Senate stated that Price Waterhouse (UK) was aware of gross irregularities in BCCI's handling of certain loans to the parent company of First American Bankshares, but failed to warn Price Waterhouse (USA) or the US regulators (Mitchell et al., 2001: 32–3).

In March 1991 Price Waterhouse was requested by the Bank of England to prepare a report on irregularities at BCCI. The document was given the code name *Sandstorm Report* and included detailed evidence of fraud by BCCI officials. The report was completed in June 1991 and led to the Bank of England closing down BCCI's operations. Although a censored version of the *Sandstorm Report* has been made available to the US Senate and is available to the American public through the Library of Congress, to date the UK government has refused to allow publication in the UK (Mitchell et al., 2001: 40–3).

Mitchell et al. (2001) argue that:

> In the banking industry, the stakeholders include not only bank depositors, but also the citizens who may ultimately be required to rescue financially distressed banks with tax subsidies and/or bear the consequences of economic disruptions caused by bank failures. Yet the audit industry does not owe any 'duty of care' to bank depositors, employees or other interested parties. In the BCCI case, the British auditors had no enforceable obligations to depositors, banking authorities, or polities outside the United Kingdom. (Mitchell et al., 2001: 49)

BCCI was effectively shut down by the Bank of England on 5 July 1991. At first, some of the media appeared to be sympathetic to the dilemma faced by the Bank of England:

> There is never a right time to close a bank. Whatever time the banking authorities around the world had pulled the plug on the Bank of Credit and Commerce International they would have been accused of acting too early or too late. But it is important to be clear about one thing: there was no alternative to shutting it down. The authorities cannot say so in public, but the real reason a further injection of funds to keep the bank running was never a serious option is this. Evidence already available suggests that the fraud goes so far up the management chain that there was no level at which BCCI could satisfy the world's banking authorities that it would be properly run. (*Independent*, 10 July 1991, Editorial: 21)

But, within days, following revelations that the Bank of England had known for some years of irregularities at BCCI, the mood in the media seemed to change. Under a headline 'The dog that didn't bark', the *Sunday Times* stated:

When the Bank of England swooped on Bank of Credit and Commerce International nine days ago, it sent shock waves around the world. On the face of it the Bank had acted with exemplary speed. And with so many discredited financiers making their way through the British courts, it looked as though there was at least one group of regulators who knew their job. The action was unprecedented in scale: assets were seized with precision timing in seven countries. Authorities in more than 60 other countries were eventually involved in what became a global operation. Secrecy was maintained up to the moment liquidators moved in to bar BCCI's doors. But any admiration won by this swift display of power slowly evaporated last week as the enormity of the affair became apparent. The fraud revealed is vast; it goes back several years and was carried out at the highest levels. (*Sunday Times*, 14 July 1991, Business Section)

DISCUSSION

The collapse of BCCI did not lead to a collapse in the Western banking system, but there were serious repercussions for a large number of individuals, employees, companies, local authorities and even sovereign governments. In the UK a large number of small Asian businesses banked with BCCI. In addition, dozens of local authorities had been attracted by the higher deposit interest rates offered by BCCI and deposited their funds with the bank. One of the worst affected was the Western Isles Council in the Outer Hebrides in Scotland which had placed $45m on deposit with BCCI. As one of the smallest local authorities in the UK this was a devastating loss.

At the time of the collapse it was estimated that around the world BCCI had 14,000 employees and over one million depositors, who would all have been affected in one way or another by the bank's collapse. Many depositors faced substantial losses. In the UK (under banking regulations) some of the smaller depositors were compensated to the extent of 75 per cent of their deposits, but only up to a maximum of £18,000.

It seems that the Bank of England faced a precarious dilemma. It knew by the summer of 1991 that BCCI was in serious trouble and there was substantial evidence of fraud. If the Bank of England tried to issue some sort of warning, there would have been a run on the bank as depositors tried to retrieve their money. Those fortunate enough to act quickly would have retrieved all their savings, with nothing left for those who acted less quickly. The Bank of England may have been hoping that the Abu Dhabi shareholders would inject sufficient capital to rescue BCCI, but appears to have decided in early July 1991 that on balance it would be better to shut down BCCI.

Moreover, the Bank of England faced the difficult task of trying to co-ordinate the actions of regulators in a number of countries in taking decisive action to close down BCCI's global operations at one go. Pakistan and Abu Dhabi clearly did not want to co-operate in this operation. It seems that the Bank of England was in an impossible situation. Evidence had been mounting for some years of irregularities at BCCI. But if the Bank of England had decided to close down BCCI in 1988 (at the time of the Tampa trial) it is likely that they would have been criticised for acting prematurely when restructuring and refinancing could have solved BCCI's problems.

It is quite possible that, in the early years of BCCI, its founder, Agha Hasan Abedi was sincere and altruistic in wanting to develop a bank that would help people in the Third World and form a bridge between developed and developing countries. It is also quite possible that Abedi and Naqvi hoped that their frauds in covering up the losses associated with Gulf Group were simply a temporary measure which would allow them a breathing space to bring BCCI back to profitability. Nevertheless, it remains an irony that although Abedi aimed to help the poorer people of the developing countries, at the end of the day they were the ones who were worst off. Abedi died in August 1995 in Karachi, Pakistan. Although a court in Abu Dhabi had served an eight-year sentence on him for fraud, the Pakistani authorities refused to allow his extradition.

Is it likely that a fraud on the scale of BCCI could be repeated? Without doubt, bank regulators will have learned some lessons from the BCCI episode. According to the *Financial Times*:

> The likelihood of there being another BCCI-style fraud is small, however. The breathtaking magnitude of BCCI's corruption was only possible because the bank operated in a vast number of different countries, each of whose regulators only had responsibility for monitoring a tiny piece in the BCCI jigsaw. (*Financial Times*, 24 October 1992: 7)

BCCI is yet another example of a breakdown in corporate governance where the repercussions are felt for many years after the initial collapse. In January 2004 in the UK High Court, the liquidators of BCCI (Deloitte) began an action which involved suing the Bank of England for losses amounting to £850m incurred in the fraud and it was estimated that the trial would last until 2006. It was also revealed that, back in 1992, Bingham had prepared a separate and secret report which looked at the role of the British intelligence services in the BCCI affair. It was reported[15] that this document revealed that the Bank of England had received numerous warnings from intelligence agencies about alleged misconduct at BCCI. So it is possible that further revelations could emerge from the BCCI saga.

Table 6.1 *BCCI: key events*

1972	Agha Hasan Abedi founds BCCI; Sheikh Zayed in Abu Dhabi agrees to provide financial support to BCCI
1982	Clark Clifford becomes chairman of First American Bankshares
1987	Price Waterhouse appointed sole auditors of BCCI
1988	Abedi has heart attack and hands over to Swaleh Naqvi; seven BCCI officials arrested in Tampa, Florida
1989	Senior employee alerts Price Waterhouse to fraud at BCCI
1990	Price Waterhouse report finds that BCCI needs additional finance of £1.8bn; Naqvi seeks additional finance in Abu Dhabi
1991	Price Waterhouse reports on fraud at BCCI (June); Bank of England shuts down BCCI branches (July)
1992	Report into BCCI by Lord Justice Bingham
2004	BCCI's liquidators (Deloitte) begin legal action in High Court against Bank of England

Discussion questions

1 Should the Bank of England have acted more promptly to shut down BCCI's operations?
2 To what extent did the complex organizational structure of BCCI assist Abedi and Naqvi in disguising the extent of the fraud at BCCI?
3 What do you believe are the main lessons that can be drawn from the revelations of fraud at BCCI?
4 Identify the stakeholders in BCCI who suffered when the bank was shut down in July 1991.
5 Should investors be concerned that a scandal similar to BCCI could be repeated in the future?

REFERENCES

Accountancy, 'When PW's concerns failed to move the Bank', December 1992: 16–17.
Adams, J.R and Frantz, D. (1993) *A Full Service Bank: How BCCI Stole Billions Around the World*. London: Simon and Schuster.
Bingham, The Right Honourable Lord Justice (1992) *Inquiry into the Supervision of the Bank of Credit and Commerce International*. London: HMSO.
Mitchell, A., Sikka, P., Arnold. P., Cooper, C., and Willmott, H. (2001) *The BCCI Cover-Up*. Basildon: Association for Accountancy and Business Affairs.

NOTES

1 *Financial Times*, 6 July 1991: 1.
2 Adams and Frantz, 1993: 14.
3 *New York Times*, 11 October 1998: 1.
4 *Independent*, 7 July 1991: 1

5 *Sunday Times*, 7 July 1991, Home News Section.

6 See Adams and Frantz, 1993: 197–9.

7 See Adams and Frantz, 1993: 263.

8 *Independent*, Business on Sunday, 25 October 1992: 4.

9 *Independent*, Business on Sunday, 25 October 1992: 4.

10 *Accountancy*, December 1992: 17.

11 *Accountancy*, December 1992: 17.

12 *Accountancy*, December 1992: 17.

13 *Sunday Times*, 25 October 1992, Business Section.

14 *Sunday Times*, 25 October 1992, Business Section.

15 *Observer*, 18 January 2004.

Enron

In 2001 Enron was one of the world's largest energy groups, operating mainly in the USA. But in that year, the company admitted that there had been a number of financial reporting irregularities over the period 1997 to 2000. During 2001 it became apparent that a number of special-purpose entities were not consolidated in the balance sheet. Consequently, earnings (reported profits) were substantially overstated and in late 2001 the company filed for Chapter 11 bankruptcy.[1]

During most of the 1990s Enron's stock price was rising steadily. During 1999 the stock price increased dramatically and at the beginning of 2000 was standing at over $70. During 2000 the stock price peaked at just over $90, but by the end of 2000 was standing at just over $80. During 2001 the stock price declined sharply and by the beginning of December 2001 the stock stood at less than $1.

Fortune magazine in early 2001 ranked Enron (on the basis of revenues) as seventh in the Fortune 500 with revenues of over $100bn. Enron during the 1990s had grown at a phenomenal pace and some analysts were already predicting that it would be number one by 2001. For seven years in a row, Enron had been ranked as *Fortune's* most innovative company.

At its peak in 2001 Enron had 30,000 employees around the world, of which 6,000 were located in Houston, Texas. The collapse of Enron was devastating for the city of Houston, since many of its inhabitants were related to employees or knew friends who worked at the company.

KENNETH LAY TAKES CHARGE

In 1985 the foundations of Enron were laid when Houston Natural Gas (where Kenneth Lay was in charge) was taken over by its larger competitor, InterNorth (also a natural-gas supplier), based in Omaha. Although he was given a lesser management role following the takeover, Lay soon became chief executive officer (CEO) and moved the headquarters from Omaha to Houston. Lay was also responsible for changing the company name to Enron with a vision 'to become the premier natural gas pipeline company in North America'. In 1990 Enron's vision was modified: 'to become the world's first natural gas major'. In 1995 the vision changed again: 'to become the world's leading energy company'. And by 2001 (ironically a few months before it was forced into bankruptcy): 'to become the world's leading company'.[2]

Kenneth Lay came to be well known in Houston for his charitable work. He also cultivated friendships with important political figures, including President G.W. Bush. Lay contributed more than $100,000 to Bush's election campaigns and Bush reportedly referred to Lay as 'Kenny Boy'.[3]

During the 1990s Enron expanded rapidly in the USA and into Central and South America, the Caribbean, India and the Philippines, and it owned a major power plant at Teesside in the north-east of England. But where Enron differed from its more traditional competitors was in terms of innovation, particularly risk management. Jeffrey Skilling had been persuaded by Kenneth Lay to move from McKinsey and Co., management consultants to Enron in 1990. Skilling was thought to be a particularly bright MBA, graduate of Harvard and reputedly the youngest partner at McKinsey. It was Skilling who was credited with creating the risk management model and Enron's strategy of 'business light', which meant an emphasis on energy and commodity trading rather than actually owning large amounts of fixed assets.

Under Skilling's guidance, Enron created weather derivatives, which allowed companies to hedge risks associated with fluctuations in weather conditions. For instance, some companies might benefit from prolonged winter conditions whereas other companies might benefit from prolonged summer conditions and high temperatures. Enron aimed to profit from companies trying to reduce their risk in such areas and began to trade weather derivatives to both types of companies. The advantage was that Enron collected premium income from companies buying the derivatives (essentially insurance) and if a particular event triggered payment, Enron calculated that the premium income would substantially exceed the payout.

Normally, Enron's risks from such transactions were limited by the fact that Enron would sell derivatives insuring against, say, warm weather, and at the same time sell derivatives insuring against cold weather. The danger would be if Enron adopted an unhedged or naked position, which was essentially a speculative bet.[4] Enron first traded derivatives in September 1997, but was keen to expand into other markets. Jeff Skilling's ambition was to focus Enron on intellectual capital and get away from physical assets. This meant that Enron's wealth was essentially locked up in its intangible assets.

With Skilling in charge, Enron was becoming the model of the new economy. He termed his strategy as one of virtual assets – meaning Enron could rule a market by dominating the market-place without owning a ton of physical assets. The Enron business was no longer about energy; it was all about risk and control of risk. It was expanding into new markets, it was *commoditizing* everything, and it was starting to move at the speed of electrons. It was a risk e-business. (Cruver, 2003: 30)

In February 2001, Lay handed over as CEO of Enron to Skilling and it was thought that Lay intended to leave business and begin a political career. Enron appeared to many to be on course to become the world's leading company.

SPECIAL PURPOSE VEHICLES (SPVs)

Andrew Fastow was Enron's chief financial officer (CFO). Fastow had been responsible for setting up three partnerships, known as LJM, LJM2 and LJM3. (The initials LJM simply happened to represent the first names of Fastow's wife, Lea, and their children.) In October 2001 the *Wall Street Journal* was to discover that the partnerships were part of the reason for the losses announced by Enron and that Fastow could receive millions of dollars from these partnerships, which were engaging in transactions with Enron.[5]

Andrew Fastow had joined Enron in 1990 and became CFO in 1998. In 1999 he was even given the Excellence Award for Capital Structure Management by *CFO Magazine* (Cruver, 2003: 127). Fastow and Michael Kopper designed partnerships that involved the creation of a trading concern called a special purpose vehicle or entity (SPV or SPE). Enron then sold an asset to the SPV. The type of asset sold to the SPV was immaterial, and in fact the asset did not even have to be moved. The SPV would pay cash for the asset and Enron could show the transaction as a sale, which would boost its reported profits.

However, the reality was that the cash received from the SPV was a loan, but by treating it as a sale, Enron benefited in two ways: firstly, its revenues and profits were increased; secondly, its debt levels were kept low. The problem was that eventually the cash would need to be repaid to the SPV. However, that payment could be deferred to a subsequent financial period when the transaction could be repeated. The problem was that the proliferation of SPVs created a highly complex system of partnerships. The deals had to be structured in such a way that they conformed to Financial Accounting Standards Board (FASB) rules and Generally Accepted Accounting Principles (GAAP). Otherwise the SPVs would have to be included in Enron's consolidated financial statements.

The following description in the *Houston Chronicle* gives some indication of the incredible complexity of these partnerships designed by Andrew Fastow:

While Enron provided descriptions of the many deals on Thursday, their complexity can be mind-numbing for anyone who isn't an accountant.

For example, in June 2000, LJM2 purchased fiber-optic cable from Enron that was installed yet unused for $30 million in cash and $70 million in an interest-bearing note, or IOU. LJM2 sold some of that fiber to other companies for $40 million, but since Enron helped market the fiber to those buyers it received an 'agency fee' of $20.3 million. In December 2000, LJM2 sold the remaining fiber for $113 million to a special entity that Enron created strictly for the purpose of that purchase. LJM2 then used some of the proceeds from the sale to pay off the $70 million Enron IOU. As if the transactions weren't complicated enough, Enron then signed a contract with one of the investors of the entity that paid $113m for the fiber to help cushion that investor from any potential losses. (*Houston Chronicle*, 9 November 2001: 1)

EXECUTIVE REMUNERATION

Apart from their salaries, Enron executives received substantial benefits. For instance, the partnership agreements were extremely lucrative for those involved and in October 2001 it was revealed that Fastow personally made $30m from these partnership transactions. It was also alleged that executives may have benefited from insider trading, that is, dealing in Enron's shares using privileged information. In October 2001 the law firm of Milberg Weiss Bershad Hynes and Lerach filed a class action law suit against Enron, alleging insider trading. Enron employees (many of whom were also Enron shareholders) were invited to join the class action which accused 29 officers and directors of insider trading. Among those named (and the proceeds of their share sales between January 2000 and October 2001) were Fastow ($33m), Lay ($184m), Skilling ($70m), Richard Causey ($13m) and Jeff McMahon ($2m).[6] Enron's bonus payments to top executives were extremely generous. In 2001 the compensation committee gave approval to plans to award 65 executives a total of $750 million for their work in 2000, which compared with Enron's net income in that year of $975 million (Useem, 2003: 246).

THE BOARD AND THE AUDIT COMMITTEE

Enron's audit committee appeared to be ineffective in preventing Enron's collapse. Of the six people on the audit committee, the independence of two members was questionable (Useem, 2003: 247). John Wakeham received annual fees of $72,000 in relation to consultancy advice to Enron's European operations. John Mendelsohn was president of a University of Texas medical centre which had received $1.6 million from Enron. Three members of the audit committee were located outside the United States: John Wakeham in the UK, Paulo Ferreira in Brazil and Ronnie Chan in Hong Kong. Finally, the chair of the audit committee, Robert Jaedicke had held the position since 1985 and in October 2001 had been cited in the Milberg Weiss Bershad Hynes and Lerach law suit as having sold Enron stock between January 2000 and October 2001 worth over $800,000 (Cruver, 2003: 131).

In 2002 the Institute of Chartered Accountants in England and Wales (ICAEW) announced that its disciplinary unit was investigating Lord Wakeham following the collapse of Enron (Reynolds, 2002: 24). Lord Wakeham had previously been a Conservative cabinet minister and had been the UK government's Secretary of State for Energy. It was presumably for his expertise on energy matters that he had been employed by Enron as a non-executive director. However, it also emerged that he had simultaneously carried out consulting work for Enron and in 2001 had received $72,000 in consulting fees.

Lord Wakeham was a non-executive director in several companies, in addition to Enron. Indeed, it was reported that at one time he sat on the boards of 16 companies, including Enron.[7] It could be argued that employees as a group were more seriously affected by the fall of Enron than were shareholders, since the employees not only lost their jobs, but found their pension entitlements were also seriously affected. John Monks, the UK Trades Union Congress general secretary, was reported as saying that 'Enron's workers have lost not just their jobs, but their pensions and savings too. The pension funds of many other US and UK workers have taken a major hit. As a member of the company's audit and compliance committee, Lord Wakeham has some very hard questions to answer. The ICAEW must ask whether its rules and standards were breached' (Reynolds, 2002: 24).

Useem (2003) comments on the board of directors and in particular the audit committee as follows:

> The board's composition thus left much to be desired if the directors were to take the right decisions when nobody was watching. It was an accounting scandal, as Sherron Watkins had warned CEO Kenneth Lay, that brought down the house, and it was thus the audit committee that was most strategically positioned to avert the disaster on behalf of the board. As its six members watched the unfolding train wreck in slow motion, they could have summoned the nerve to challenge their engineers before it was too late. Yet their remote locations, their dependence on management, and the chair's duration at the helm all contributed to an audit committee whose decisions proved lethal. (Useem, 2003: 247)

SHERRON WATKINS – WHISTLEBLOWER

In mid-2001, Sherron Watkins, an accountant at Enron, was becoming increasingly alarmed about the use of off-balance sheet financing schemes. In June 2001 Watkins was working for Andrew Fastow and came across a number of entities (known by Enron staff as 'Raptors') that were hiding losses amounting to hundreds of millions of dollars. At first it seemed that the Raptors were simply part of a hedging strategy, but eventually it became clear that their purpose was to keep losses and debt away from the published financial statements. Moreover, the Raptors were capitalized by Enron stock, and as Enron's stock price fell during 2001, Enron had to add more stock.[8] Watkins believed that Enron was a 'disaster waiting to happen' and decided to look for another job.[9]

Watkins was reluctant to confront her immediate boss, Fastow, about the ventures and decided to approach Skilling instead. However, Skilling abruptly resigned on 14 August 2001 and the following day Watkins decided to send an anonymous memo to Kenneth Lay, outlining her concerns. Although the memo was anonymous, it would probably not have been difficult for the senior management to draw up a shortlist of potential suspects who might have sent it. Watkins even revealed in the memo that she had worked at Enron for eight years. Months later, following Enron's bankruptcy, the memo was revealed in the media and Watkins became widely regarded as a whistleblower and even a heroine who had tried to prevent Enron's collapse. Certainly, it must have taken some courage to take her concerns to the top of the organization and incur all the unwelcome attention that goes with being a 'whistleblower'.

Extracts from Sherron Watkins' anonymous memo to Enron CEO Ken Lay (15 August 2001)

Dear Mr Lay,

Has Enron become a risky place to work? For those of us who didn't get rich over the last few years, can we afford to stay?

Skilling's abrupt departure will raise suspicions of accounting improprieties and valuation issues. Enron has been very aggressive in its accounting – most notably the Raptor transactions and the Condor vehicle. We do have valuation issues with our international assets and possibly some of our EES MTM positions.

The spotlight will be on us, the market just can't accept that Skilling is leaving his dream job. I think that the valuation issues can be fixed and reported with other goodwill write-downs to occur in 2002. How do we fix the Raptor and Condor deals? They unwind in 2002 and 2003, we will have to pony up Enron stock and that won't go unnoticed.

I am incredibly nervous that we will implode in a wave of accounting scandals. My 8 years of Enron work history will be worth nothing on my resumé, the business world will consider the past successes as nothing but an elaborate accounting hoax. Skilling is resigning now 'for personal reasons' but I think he wasn't having fun, looked down the road and knew this stuff was unfixable and would rather abandon ship now than resign in shame in 2 years time.

Is there a way our accounting guru's can unwind these deals now? I have thought and thought about how to do this, but I keep bumping into one big problem – we booked the Condor and Raptor deals in 1999 and 2000, we enjoyed a wonderfully high stock price, many executives sold stock, we then try and reverse or fix the deals in 2001 and it's a bit like robbing the bank in one year and trying to pay it back 2 years later. Nice try, but investors were hurt, they bought at $70 and $80/share looking for $120/share and now they're at $38 or worse. We are under too much scrutiny and there are probably one or two disgruntled "redeployed" employees who know enough about the "funny" accounting to get us into trouble.

What do we do? I know this question cannot be addressed in the all employee meeting, but can you give some assurances that you and Causey will sit down and take a good hard objective look at what is going to happen to Condor and Raptor in 2002 and 2003? (Swartz with Watkins, 2003, pp. 361–2)

The memo itself makes interesting reading (see extracts). Watkins did manage to arrange a meeting with Lay on 22 August 2001 and subsequently wrote a number of further memos to him. In one, Watkins repeated a comment she had heard from another manager: 'I know it would be devastating to all of us, but I wish we would get caught. We're such a crooked company'.[10] In another memo Watkins advised that a law firm should be hired to investigate the Condor and Raptor transactions. However, she advised against using Enron's law firm Vinson and Elkins, who would have a conflict of interest since they had had some involvement in the Raptor transactions.

As a result of Watkins' memo and meeting on 22 August 2001, Kenneth Lay did seek outside legal advice, but unfortunately he chose to approach Enron's lawyers, Vinson and Elkins, which Watkins had specifically advised against.

By 29 August 2001, Fastow had discovered that Sherron Watkins was the author of the anonymous memo of 15 August and wanted her fired. Kenneth Lay's reaction was to tell Fastow that he was not going to promote him to chief operating officer, but instead would launch an investigation into the SPVs.

Two partners from Vinson and Elkins submitted their report on 15 October 2001, but the overall thrust of their report was that there was nothing fundamentally wrong at Enron. They stated that 'the facts disclosed through our preliminary investigation do not, in our judgement, warrant a further widespread investigation by independent counsel and auditors ... the accounting treatment on the Condor/Whitewing and Raptor transactions is creative and aggressive, but no one has reason to believe that it is inappropriate from a technical standpoint'.[11]

ENRON'S CASH CRISIS

In February 2001 Jeff Skilling had taken over from Kenneth Lay as chief executive officer. This had been widely expected for a number of years and it meant that in early 2001 Kenneth Lay was chairman with Jeff Skilling as president and CEO. Just six months later (14 August 2001) Enron employees were surprised to learn that Skilling would resign from Enron.

An e-mail from Kenneth Lay to Enron staff stated that Skilling's resignation was for personal reasons and that it was voluntary. Enron's share price had been falling in recent weeks, but Lay continued optimistically:

> With Jeff leaving, the Board has asked me to resume the responsibilities of President and CEO in addition to my role as Chairman of the Board. I have agreed. I want to assure you that I have never felt better about the prospects for the company. All of you know that our stock price has suffered substantially over the last few months. One of my top priorities will be to restore a significant amount of the stock value we have lost as soon as possible. Our performance has never been stronger; our business model has never been more robust; our growth has never been more certain; and most importantly, we have never had a better nor deeper pool of talent throughout the company. We have the finest organization in American business today. Together, we will make Enron the world's leading company. (Cruver, 2003: 91)

At one point in September 2001, when Enron was desperately seeking sources of cash, it was thought that a wealthy equity investor might be able to help save the company. Three Enron executives flew to Omaha to see if Warren Buffet, the well-known head of Berkshire Hathaway, would be prepared to invest in Enron. Buffet's apparent response was that he was not interested and would only invest in businesses that he could understand.[12]

During October 2001 Enron was becoming desperate to negotiate additional credit, although the company was trying to maintain in public that its trading was strong. Credit agencies such as Moody's Investors Service began to downgrade Enron's debt and, as a result of the lower credit ratings, Enron's financing costs increased and lenders demanded early repayment.

It is not easy to pinpoint a particular date when Enron began to fall apart, but mid-October 2001 was certainly a critical time. The *Wall Street Journal* stated that Enron was reporting a third-quarter loss of $618m after $1.01 billion in charges 'that reflect risks it has taken in transforming itself from a pipeline company into a diversified trading company'.[13] The newspaper also reported that some of the charges related to partnerships run by Andrew Fastow, which raised questions over a possible conflict of interest.

From mid-October a series of media revelations were responsible for

Enron's share price going into serious decline. On 19 October 2001 the *Wall Street Journal* reported that Kenneth Lay had made $7 million in management fees from one of the partnerships in one year.[14] On 23 October 2001, when Enron's share price stood at just over $20, the *Wall Street Journal* reported:

> While Enron was riding high, its often difficult-to-understand reports were generally not seen as being a problem. The company appeared to be the dominant force in the business of energy trading, and to produce phenomenal profits. When Mr. Lay was reported as having played an important role in formulating the Bush administration's energy policies, the aura was only enhanced. In January, the shares traded for $84. But now, with some of the company's ventures clearly having run into problems, it appears that investors are growing less willing to accept the company's reports. That the partnership transactions were disclosed at all was because of the involvement of the chief financial officer, and some have wondered if there might have been similar deals with others. (*Wall Street Journal*, 23 October 2001, Section C: 1)

On 24 October 2001 Andrew Fastow resigned as chief financial officer. On 8 November 2001, Enron announced that it had found errors amounting to $600m going back nearly five years. The group was having to restate its finances as far back as 1997 to account for the losses, which related to some complex partnerships now under investigation by the Securities and Exchange Commission. Enron announced that it had fired a number of employees who had invested in the partnerships (one of the employees being Andrew Fastow). Kenneth Lay maintained that the release of the information was intended 'to calm the concerns of shareholders and federal investigators'.[15] Another view by one analyst at the time was that 'At the end of the day these details give support to the fear that Enron was a financial house of cards . . . it would make a good case study on what happens when you fly too close to the sun'.[16]

In October 2001 Kenneth Lay had begun negotiations with Dynegy, a smaller competitor in the energy industry. Lay believed that Enron could be saved if Dynegy took over Enron, leaving Kenneth Lay to retire gracefully. On 9 November 2001, Dynegy announced that it had agreed to buy its larger rival, Enron. However, part of the price of the deal was that if the takeover did not proceed, Dynegy would gain control of one of Enron's main assets, the Northern Natural Gas pipeline.

Lay's contract stipulated that, in the event of Enron being sold, he would be entitled to $20 million for each year remaining on his contract. Since his contract still had three years to run, this meant that Lay would be entitled to compensation of $60 million. In mid-November it appeared that Lay was keen to exercise his rights under the contract but, after a meeting with some of Enron's energy traders, he was persuaded to change his mind.[17]

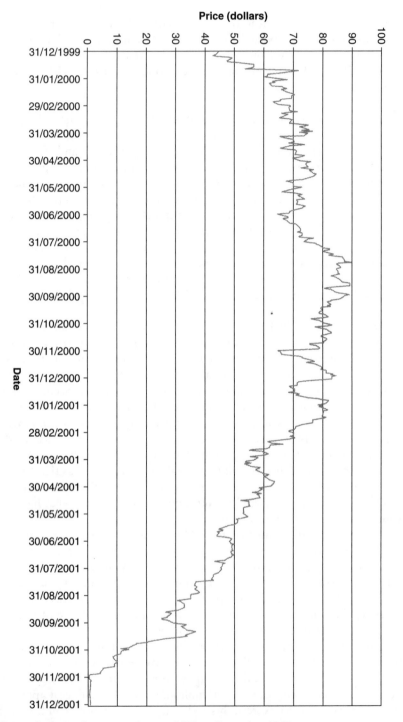

Figure 2 Enron share price, January 2000 to December 2002

Source: Datastream

The takeover of Enron by Dynegy did not go smoothly. During November 2001 Enron's share price continued to fall, not helped by the fact that on 14 November Enron announced that it was trying to raise an additional $500 million to $1 billion of equity and on November 19 Enron restated its third-quarter earnings. Finally, on 28 November 2001 Dynegy decided to withdraw from its takeover of Enron, complaining that Enron had not fully informed Dynegy of its precarious financial position. Enron's share price fell below $1. On 2 December 2001 Enron filed for Chapter 11 bankruptcy protection.

Even in the final weeks before Enron's bankruptcy, it seems that Enron employees could not believe that Enron would collapse and were actually buying Enron shares as the price fell. On 3 December Enron dismissed about 4,000 employees at its Houston headquarters. In addition 1,100 employees had been dismissed in Europe in the previous week. Enron employees also suffered because the value of their pension plans fell and it was estimated that the retirement plans had lost about $1.2 billion dollars in 2001 because of the fall in Enron's stock price. Employees were told that they could expect $4,500 in severance pay, no matter how many years they had been employed with Enron.[18]

CONSEQUENCES OF ENRON'S COLLAPSE

In September 2004 Enron was allowed to sell its interest in three natural-gas pipelines and Portland General Electric for $3.1bn, with the purchasers assuming about $1.5bn of Enron's debt. As a result of these transactions, the remnants of Enron were due to be restructured as Prisma Energy International Inc., with almost 5,000 employees. Prisma was destined to own a mixture of pipeline and power assets in 14 countries, many in Latin America. It was expected that Enron would distribute $12 billion to its 20,000 creditors, 92 per cent in cash and the remaining 8 per cent in Prisma stock. This meant that Enron's creditors would receive about 20 per cent of the $63bn they were owed, but the shareholders would receive nothing.[19]

The major audit firm Arthur Andersen became one of the casualties of the Enron collapse. In July 2002 Arthur Andersen had over $9bn of turnover in 2001, with a 'reputation for outstanding auditing integrity and competence'.[20] But by the end of 2002, Arthur Andersen as an audit firm was effectively finished with its workforce reduced from 85,000 to 3,000 and barred from auditing in the USA.

Speaking in 2004, Sherron Watkins said 'I don't see a sea change where corporations welcome whistleblowers . . . Whistleblowing is just a bad name'.[21] Despite the fact that legal protection for corporate whistleblowers is now included in Sarbanes–Oxley and protection may be available in future for whistleblowers under company legislation in the UK, whistleblowers are not often popular with companies. Although the media has in general gone out of its way to praise Sherron Watkins as a heroine of the

Enron saga, she is quite modest about her role at Enron. 'Certainly I didn't make any difference at Enron. Maybe in subsequent prosecutions but not in saving the company. When Lay picked a law firm which had actually approved part of the structures used in the fraud to look into my concerns, I should have realised he was going to do a whitewash investigation. With hindsight I should have gone to the audit committee'.[22] However, she believes she has raised awareness of the issues and the additional protection afforded under Sarbanes–Oxley may make it easier for whistleblowers in the future.

Other casualties of the Enron saga included JP Morgan Chase and Citigroup, which were each fined nearly $300m for deals with Enron, and Merrill Lynch, which was fined $80m for a transaction on which it made a profit of only $500,000. Watkins believes that a fundamental issue in cases such as Enron is ethics and her advice is 'Don't stay with a company that isn't ethical because something like an Enron could happen to you'. Watkins' view of Arthur Andersen is that there was too much emphasis on unrealistically high levels of pay. 'I hate to sound simplistic but it all comes down to power and money corrupting people. Greed breeds more greed'. 'The biggest mistake would be to think that Enron is an aberration, that it couldn't happen somewhere else. People think it was obvious; that it was a house of cards and that we all should have seen it, but we didn't'.[23]

DISCUSSION

Deakin and Konzelmann (2004: 136) argue that part of Enron's problems could be attributed to its decision to become involved in derivatives trades, particularly in markets such as broadband. These markets were extremely volatile and Enron had no physical presence and no specialized knowledge that could give the company a comparative advantage. It is possible that, in future, investors and stakeholders will take greater notice of credit ratings provided by credit rating agencies, which can give an indication of financial risk.

Enron was known as a very competitive company, which rewarded its staff with high salaries and large bonuses, but at the same time used aggressive job evaluation and firing policies. The company professed to espouse respect, integrity, communication and excellence (RICE) as its core values, but the reality was in fact quite different:

> The contrast between Enron's moral mantra and the behavior of some Enron executives is bone-chilling. Indeed, the Enron saga teaches us the limitations of corporate codes of ethics: how empty and ineffectual they can be. Long touted as crucial accoutrements to moral rectitude, codes are useless when the words are hollow – when executives lack either the dedication to espoused virtues or the ability to make defensible ethical decisions.[24]

The conduct of the board of directors has also been criticized:

> Enron directors had raised too few questions and challenged too few assumptions during its many meetings with management. It was a board that routinely relied on Enron executives and Andersen partners for information but took scant effort to verify it. The board quickly approved management's risky steps and illicit partnerships, and then exercised too little oversight of the execution that followed. (Useem, 2003: 248)

As regards the auditors, Arthur Andersen had carried out both audit and non-audit services, giving rise to a potential conflict of interest. For instance, the audit part of Arthur Andersen would be reluctant to upset Enron's management, because that would risk losing not just the audit services, but also the lucrative non-audit services (such as management consulting work). In 2001, the firm of Arthur Andersen had received from Enron $25m for audit services and $27m for non-audit services. Arthur Andersen also acted illegally by shredding and deleting documents, and in May 2002 the lead auditor admitted to obstruction of justice (Squires et al., 2003: 16). The repercussions for Arthur Andersen were severe. Public companies lost confidence in Arthur Andersen and went to other firms of accountants for their audit services. The audit side of Arthur Andersen simply folded, although the management consultancy division was rebranded as Accenture.

Ben Glisan, former Treasurer at Enron, became the first executive to be sentenced to prison after pleading guilty to criminal fraud and admitting to manipulating Enron's financial statements. He was sentenced to five years in federal prison and also faced a fine of over $900,000. Like many Enron employees, Glisan had worked at Arthur Andersen before joining Enron. At Enron he worked with Andrew Fastow and Michael Kopper to devise partnership schemes that would allow billions of dollars in debt to be removed from Enron's balance sheet.[25] Kopper had pleaded guilty in August 2002 to a number of criminal charges connected with Enron. In January 2004 Fastow pleaded guilty to two counts of conspiracy.

In July 2004, Lay was indicted on eleven criminal counts of securities and bank fraud,[26] but he was still positive about what Enron had stood for:

> We were doing some very exciting things. We were changing markets. We were changing the way people bought and sold energy, bought and sold a lot of other things. And we were changing the risk management of many different areas, all the way from weather derivatives to ways to hedge oil prices or gas prices or coal prices. We were providing cleaner fuel around the world. We were on the cutting edge of really pushing natural gas – the use of natural gas – instead of coal and oil. And we were pushing renewable energy. (*Financial Times Magazine*, 7 August 2004: 15)

Apart from the court trials which involved Lay, Skilling, Fastow and others, the US authorities began to take action against Enron's bankers. In September 2004, at the Southern US District Court in Houston, charges were laid against four ex-Merrill Lynch bankers. Along with two Enron executives, they faced fraud charges in connection with the sale of three Nigerian electricity generating barges to Merrill Lynch in 1999. The prosecution case was that Enron's transfer of interest in the three barges was in fact a sham sale designed to inflate the company's earnings by $12m and generate bonuses for those involved in the transaction. Although the sums involved were relatively small compared to Enron's overall losses, the trial outcome might help to define the extent to which the financial community had been aware of or even assisted Enron with its off-balance-sheet financing arrangements.[27] The prosecution case was that in a subsequent financial reporting period Enron would buy back the barges from Merrill Lynch, which would be guaranteed a profit on the deal. In other words, the transaction in reality amounted to a loan, rather than sale of assets.

A good deal of information has now emerged from the Enron saga, particularly relating to the events of Enron's chaotic final months in 2001. Nevertheless, given that court cases are still pending against the main actors such as Lay and Skilling, it could be years before a full and definitive version of events can be compiled.

Table 7.1 *Enron: key events*

1985	InterNorth takes over Houston Natural Gas
1987	Merged company changes name to Enron; Kenneth Lay becomes CEO
1989	Enron begins trading natural gas
1990	Jeff Skilling moves from McKinsey & Co. to Enron
1994	Enron begins trading electricity
1996	Jeff Skilling appointed president and chief operating officer
1997	Enron begins trading weather derivatives
February 2001	Jeff Skilling becomes CEO
August 2001	Jeff Skilling resigns as CEO; Ken Lay takes over as CEO and president (and retains his role as chairman); Watkins sends anonymous memo to Lay
October 2001	Enron reports third-quarter loss of $618 million; Andrew Fastow resigns over partnership deals
November 2001	Dynegy announces agreement to take over Enron; nineteen days later Dynegy pulls out of agreement
December 2001	Enron files for Chapter 11 bankruptcy protection
2004	Enron is restructured as Prisma Energy International

Discussion questions

1 Discuss the relative risks of companies with substantial physical assets compared with companies which have substantial intangible assets.

2 The phrases 'train crash' and 'house of cards' have been used by commentators to describe Enron's collapse. Do you believe these analogies are useful in this case?

3 If Enron shareholders had been fully aware of the LJM partnership agreements, do you believe they would have been willing to continue investing in Enron?

4 Discuss the potential problems with Kenneth Lay taking over as CEO and president in August 2001 (as well as continuing to be chairman).

5 Identify the stakeholders who suffered as a result of the Enron bankruptcy.

6 Discuss whether potential whistleblowers should be encouraged to report their concerns of poor corporate governance. Should they report their concerns within or outside the organization?

7 What particular features about Enron's board of directors reduced the likelihood that the company's problems would be properly addressed?

REFERENCES

Blyth, A. (2003) 'Get over it', *Accountancy*, February: 35–7.

Cruver, B. (2003) *Enron: Anatomy of Greed*. London: Arrow Books.

Deakin, S. and Konzelmann, S.J. (2004) 'Learning from Enron', *Corporate Governance: An International Review*, Vol. 12, No. 2: 134–42.

Reynolds, B. (2002) 'ICAEW investigates Lord Wakeham over Enron', *Accountancy*, October: 24.

Squires, S.E., Smith, C.J., McDougall, L. and Yeack, W.R. (2003) *Inside Arthur Andersen: Shifting Values, Unexpected Consequences*. New Jersey: Financial Times Prentice Hall.

Swartz, M. with Watkins, S. (2003) *Power Failure: The Rise and Fall of Enron*. London: Aurum Press.

Useem, M. (2003) 'Corporate governance is directors making decisions: reforming the outward foundations for inside decision making', *Journal of Management and Governance*, Vol. 7: 241–53.

NOTES

1 Under US regulations there are two types of bankruptcy arrangement: Chapter 7 bankruptcy is the most severe and effectively implies almost immediate liquidation of a company's assets; Chapter 11 bankruptcy allows the firm some respite from its creditors while it tries to refinance and restructure.

2 See Cruver, 2003: 21–2.

3 *Financial Times*, 10 July 2004: 15.

4 Barings Bank was brought down in spectacular fashion in 1995 by Nick Leeson, who traded unhedged derivatives.

5 *Wall Street Journal*, 17 October 2001, Section C: 1.

6 Cruver, 2003: 130–1.

7 *Financial Times*, 27 April 2002: 14

8 See Swartz with Watkins, 2003: 269–70.

9 Swartz with Watkins, 2003: 270.

10 Swartz with Watkins, 2003: 367.

11 Swartz with Watkins, 2003: 304.

12 See Swartz with Watkins, 2003: 330–1.

13 *Wall Street Journal*, 17 October 2001: 1.
14 Swartz with Watkins, 2003: 308.
15 *Houston Chronicle*, 9 November 2001: 1.
16 *Houston Chronicle*, 9 November 2001: 1.
17 Swartz with Watkins, 2003: 333.
18 *New York Times*, 4 December 2001, Business Section: 1.
19 Associated Press, 10 September 2004, Business News.
20 Blyth, 2003: 35.
21 *Accountancy*, January 2004: 64–5.
22 *Accountancy*, January 2004: 64.
23 *Accountancy*, January 2004: 64.
24 S. Salbu, Foreword to *Enron: Anatomy of Greed* by B. Cruver (2003).
25 *Financial Times*, 11 September 2003: 29.
26 *Financial Times*, 10 July 2004: 15.
27 *Financial Times*, 20 September 2004: 20.

WorldCom

WorldCom filed for Chapter 11 bankruptcy protection in July 2002. The previous March, the US Securities and Exchange Commission had begun an investigation into accounting irregularities at the company. In 2002 WorldCom had admitted to misclassifying substantial capital expenditures in previous periods. In March 2004 Bernie Ebbers, the former chief executive officer (CEO), was charged with fraud, conspiracy and making false statements in connection with the accounting irregularities that led to WorldCom's collapse. Scott Sullivan, the former chief financial officer (CFO) had previously agreed to plead guilty to similar charges and testify against his former boss, Bernie Ebbers.[1]

The consequences of the bankruptcy were severe for shareholders, who lost virtually all their investments, and many employees lost their jobs. Creditors also lost out. However, the company did emerge from bankruptcy in May 2004 and was renamed MCI.

BERNIE EBBERS' EARLY BUSINESS LIFE

Born in Edmonton in Canada in 1941, Ebbers spent his early years there and enrolled at the University of Alberta, but left after one year. Several years later he enrolled at Mississippi College in the United States and graduated in 1967 with a degree in physical education. In later life he was grateful for the education he had received at Mississippi College and was very generous to it in terms of financial support. Ebbers married in 1968 and for several years did a variety of jobs, including coaching basketball at a local high school and working in a garment manufacturing company. After a few years he left the garment factory to buy a motel and restaurant.

In his early business career, Ebbers acquired a reputation for being careful with business expenses and being skilful in making deals. He bought more motels and successfully built up a sizeable motel chain, Master Corporation. His early business model was based on the theory that a motel could double in value after five years and in the meantime aim to show a reasonable operating profit. But in 1983 another business opportunity presented itself. In that year, a court ruling ordered AT&T's Bell System to allow competition in the long-distance telephone market. AT&T was forced to lease long-distance phone lines to small regional companies, who could then sell the capacity on to other users.

Ebbers met up with a few other associates who agreed to set up a company reselling telecom services in 1983. The new firm's name was agreed as Long Distance Discount Services (LDDS). Ebbers was one of nine initial subscribers to the equity, taking 14.5 per cent of the share capital, but he chose not to join the original board of directors. Even at that time Ebbers was not entirely convinced about the possibilities for reselling telecom services at a profit and creating a successful company with good growth prospects, but he was persuaded by his associates to participate in the venture.

LONG DISTANCE DISCOUNT SERVICES (LDDS)

LDDS began operations in January 1984 with 200 customers. At first LDDS had neither sufficient technical expertise nor the right technical equipment (such as switching facilities) to win over larger and more profitable companies. In order to grow the company, LDDS needed to invest in equipment and properly trained technical staff, but this was expensive and the company was soon struggling financially. By the end of 1984 LDDS had accumulated debts of about $1.5 million.

Because Ebbers had proved himself as a shrewd businessman in running his motel chain, it was decided by the board of LDDS that it would be useful to ask him to take charge and in 1985 Ebbers became CEO. Within a few months Ebbers was able to turn the company round and turn it into a profitable business. When he took up his equity stake in LDDS, Ebbers' original intention was simply to remain as an investor and concentrate on his motel business. But when LDDS began to flounder, he decided that he should put his efforts into rescuing the telecoms business.

Ebbers acquired a reputation for being good at keeping costs under control. He also managed to keep staff numbers down but at the same time increase revenues. Although he was not a telecommunications expert, he developed a good understanding of the industry and its prospects and he proved to be a very competent, if sometimes abrasive, manager. He seemed to be able to inspire loyalty in many of his employees. For them, this could mean working extremely long hours to make LDDS successful, though he could also be a benevolent employer.

Ebbers was a devout Christian and for a number of years led Sunday bible classes at his local Baptist church. One account referred to the public image of him as easy-going and God-fearing, but those who dealt with him on a daily basis were aware of his rages over petty details. At times he could be confrontational but at other times extremely compassionate.

At board and stockholder meetings, Ebbers always led meetings with a prayer, a tradition that especially endeared older Mississippians, many of whom had invested their life savings in WorldCom stock and doled out starter shares for weddings, anniversaries, graduations, and birthdays. They didn't realize that Ebbers was known to stay up drinking half the night with colleagues, even before board meetings. Some Mississippians had a cultlike devotion to Ebbers and stubbornly held onto their stock until it was virtually worthless. But the Christian basis for the company was slowly eroding and so was Ebbers' demeanor. As his power increased and the trappings of success grew abundant, he dismissed obstacles, or what some former executives referred to as his 'Christian conscience'. (Jeter, 2003: 91)

Nevertheless, he appreciated that economies of scale were crucial to LDDS's success, especially given the highly competitive nature of the industry. LDDS therefore embarked on an ambitious expansion programme, through acquisitions and mergers, that would last for the next 15 years. In a relatively short time LDDS, with Ebbers as CEO, had grown very quickly and by 1988 sales were $95 million. In order to maintain this rate of growth and the strategy of expansion, Ebbers realized that the company would have to get a stock market quotation to gain access to the necessary finance. A suitable opportunity presented itself when a NASDAQ listed company, Advantage Companies Inc. (ACI), was facing bankruptcy and LDDS acquired it in 1989.

Charles Cannada was appointed CFO of LDDS in 1989. In 1992 Scott Sullivan became vice president and assistant treasurer, reporting to Cannada and in 1994 Sullivan was promoted to CFO. Sullivan, who had worked at KPMG, was, according to some accounts, a workaholic and was said to frequently work 20-hour days. Although Ebbers and Sullivan got on very well together, Sullivan seemed to irritate divisional managers.[2]

LDDS became increasingly aggressive in its takeover and merger strategy. Although he was head of a technology company, Ebbers was the first to admit that he was not a technical expert. And it has been reported that while CEO at LDDS and later WorldCom, Ebbers was reluctant to use the internet and preferred to send handwritten faxes. Nevertheless it seems clear that in the late 1980s he understood the importance of installing networks with large bandwidth to carry data. During the early 1990s, LDDS continued to grow by leasing lines wholesale and reselling at attractive discounted retail prices. LDDS continued to make acquisitions in 1992 and 1993. The company began to expand into California and the north-east United States, as well as Europe, and was looking to expand into South America. In 1995, LDDS took over one of its major suppliers, WilTel, leading to cost savings and synergy gains. In May 1995, LDDS was renamed WorldCom, which underlined the ambitious global intentions of both the company and Ebbers.

WorldCom's entry into the internet market was considerably helped by the purchase of UUNET Technologies, which was headed by John Sidgmore when it was taken over in 1996 by MFS Communications Company. Within weeks, WorldCom took over MFS and Sidgmore joined WorldCom to head its internet division. In 1996, the *Wall Street Journal* ranked WorldCom as number one in terms of shareholder return over the previous decade.

WORLDCOM TAKES OVER MCI

In Britain, the Telecommunications Act of 1996 had largely deregulated the industry with the intention of increasing competition and driving down prices for consumers. However, the most obvious result of the Act seemed to be a wave of takeovers and mergers. In 1997 British Telecom (BT) was in the process of discussing a takeover of MCI. At that time this would have constituted the largest foreign investment in a US company. Even though BT and MCI were each much larger than WorldCom, Sullivan reasoned that a takeover of MCI by WorldCom was feasible. In fact, it seemed that synergy gains for WorldCom could be very large, given WorldCom's own telecommunications network.

WorldCom was able to outbid BT for MCI, even though BT was already holding a 20 per cent stake in MCI. WorldCom had to pay cash for BT's stake in MCI, but WorldCom was able to issue its own equity to gain the necessary control of MCI. WorldCom would have preferred to complete the deal without purchasing the BT stake in cash. An all-equity takeover would have given WorldCom a stronger case for accounting for the takeover as a 'pooling of interests' merger, rather than using the acquisition method. The 'pooling of interests' method of group accounting was allowed at that time in the USA and would not have created goodwill on the balance sheet.[3] On the other hand, the acquisition method would create goodwill and this would have adverse implications for reported profits in the future.[4]

The entire deal, however, underlined the value of having a highly rated share price. In this respect it was important that the price of WorldCom shares held up and Jack Grubman, an analyst with Salomon Smith Barney, was noticeable for being an enthusiastic supporter of WorldCom shares. At that time the takeover of MCI by WorldCom was the largest takeover in history, but in the USA this was a time of almost frenzied merger and acquisitions activity and within months that particular record had already been overtaken.

WORLDCOM'S SHARE PRICE PEAKS

At its peak in 1999 WorldCom's market capitalization was $115 billion; it was the 14th largest company in the United States and 24th largest in the world.[5] WorldCom and MCI had two different business cultures. In MCI ideas were encouraged from junior staff, but at WorldCom new ideas tended to be initiated by senior management and Ebbers, Sullivan and Sidgmore were seen as the three most important people in terms of making deals and seeing through takeovers.

Then the opportunity to take over Nextel presented itself. This move would have broadened WorldCom's presence in the internet business and was strongly supported by Sidgmore, but opposed by Sullivan. At first Ebbers backed Sidgmore, but when Sullivan protested, Ebbers decided to back Sullivan, presumably because Ebbers felt that Sullivan's expertise was irreplaceable. From then on, Sidgmore's role and participation at WorldCom declined although he still remained vice-chairman.

The WorldCom takeover of MCI was finally completed in 1998 and in that year WorldCom also took over two major companies, Brooks Fiber and CompuServe. Sidgmore could take much of the credit for moving WorldCom from outdated telephone technology into modern data communications. Sullivan could claim much of the credit for seeing that the takeover of MCI was possible and in 1998 Sullivan received the CFO Excellence Award for mergers and acquisitions from *CFO Magazine*.[6]

WorldCom continued to acquire companies. In 1999, WorldCom began talks with Sprint, a large telecoms provider in the USA. However, it was about this time that internet growth started to decline and the telecommunications industry was becoming increasingly competitive. WorldCom found it difficult to maintain the profit margin it had obtained during most of the 1990s. Although WorldCom shareholders agreed the takeover of Sprint in April 2000, regulators in the USA and Europe ruled that such a merger would be anticompetitive.

In June 2000 the US Justice Department blocked the deal and Ebbers decided not to contest the decision in the courts. The abandonment of the merger coincided with a fall in WorldCom's share price and rumours began that WorldCom itself might be subject to a takeover bid.[7] The collapse of the Sprint deal meant that WorldCom would not be able to quickly expand into modern bandwith technology and would not be able to reduce its relative exposure to traditional voice telecommunications.

The start of WorldCom's decline can probably be traced to the period of the abortive Sprint deal and the decline in popularity of TMT (technology, media and telecommunications) stocks. In June 1999 WorldCom's share price had peaked at $62 but a year later it was standing at $46. The market seemed to sense that WorldCom's growth had been made on the back of its ambitious acquisitions programme. Once that halted, the share price would level off or begin to decline. As soon as WorldCom began to revise downwards its growth prospects, its share price began to fall.

To add to WorldCom's problems, complaints began to surface about WorldCom's level of customer service. During the 1990s, WorldCom had been acquiring a steady stream of companies. But the company had not stopped to consider properly integrating each company into the overall

WorldCom structure. Each telecoms acquisition had a different technical structure, different billing structure and different sales plans. Law suits initiated by irate customers in 2000 and 2001 were eventually settled by WorldCom agreeing to pay substantial penalties and refunds. In 2001 WorldCom agreed to pay $88 million in refunds to settle a class action lawsuit that accused Worldcom of dropping millions of customers from its existing calling plans and charging them higher casual caller rates. And in March 2002 WorldCom agreed to pay $8.5 million in penalties and refunds to settle state charges that it tricked some Californians into signing up for long-distance services and billed others for charges without permission.[8]

WORLDCOM'S LOANS TO EBBERS

In the late 1990s Ebbers' personal spending was beginning to climb. In July 1998 he bought a ranch in British Columbia for an estimated $66 million. He also acquired a yacht. In 1999 a private company in which he had a 65 per cent stake paid about $400 million for timberland in Alabama, Mississippi and Tennessee.[9] In 2002 it was learned that WorldCom had made loans to Ebbers amounting to $341 million. Interest payable by Ebbers on these loans was about 2.16 per cent, which was lower than the cost to WorldCom of actually borrowing the money. So why should the board of WorldCom adopt such a generous lending policy towards its CEO?

One possible explanation was a concern that Ebbers might be forced to sell large amounts of his shareholdings in WorldCom to resolve his personal financial problems and this could have a negative impact on WorldCom's share price:

> Why does this financially strapped telecom give its CEO such a huge gift? WorldCom was worried that Ebbers, who speculated in tech companies, might have a margin call on the shares he owned in WorldCom. If they were dumped in a forced sale, it could set off a panic that would further pummel the price of WorldCom stock. So the board loaned Ebbers the money to protect his personal holdings. This is capitalism at its finest. If the CEO's investments are successful, he wins. If they fail, the company loses. (*New York Daily News*, 25 March 2002: 38)

Ebbers' position as CEO was becoming untenable. At the beginning of April 2002, WorldCom was forced to announce that 3,700 US-based staff would be made redundant. At the end of April, Ebbers resigned and Sidgmore was named as vice-chairman, president and chief executive officer. The *New York Times* summed up WorldCom's problems as follows:

The move reflects both WorldCom's particular woes and the broader turmoil in the telecommunications sector, where earnings have been decimated by overinvestment in networks and business has yet to rebound from the recession. Many of the troubled companies had turbo-charged their growth in the 1990's with expensive acquisitions that have proved hard to blend together. (*New York Times*, 2 May 2002: 1)

CYNTHIA COOPER AND THE INTERNAL AUDIT

In 2001, internal auditors were beginning to find problems with WorldCom's accounting of sales commissions. In June 2001, a report to the WorldCom board stated that overpayment on sales commissions had totalled $930,000.[10] In March 2002, internal auditor Cynthia Cooper reported some dubious accounting transactions to the audit committee. These related to apparently ordinary operating expenses which had been treated as capital investment. That is, instead of writing off the expenses immediately in the profit-and-loss account (thereby reducing reported profit), WorldCom was capitalizing some items and writing them off to the profit-and-loss account over a much longer period. The audit committee failed to act on this information.[11] This was to become a crucial issue at WorldCom and an important contributor to its decline in share price. If the audit committee and the board had acted more quickly, then confidence in WorldCom's accounts might have been maintained.

Cynthia Cooper, the internal auditor, was finding it difficult to get a satisfactory explanation from Scott Sullivan for the expenses that had been accounted for as capital expenditure. In May 2002 Sidgmore sacked Arthur Andersen as WorldCom's auditors and hired KPMG in their place. On 13 June 2002, Cynthia Cooper reported her findings on the accounting to the head of the board of directors' audit committee. Sullivan was asked to justify his accounting procedures in a written statement at a meeting that included Arthur Andersen and KPMG. Sullivan tried to defend his accounting for line costs (as capital expenditure rather than profit-and-loss expense items). Arthur Andersen professed not to have been consulted about this particular accounting treatment and could not explain why their audit had not brought this problem to light.[12]

Sullivan was sacked as CFO on 24 June 2002. Two days later it was reported that WorldCom had overstated its cash flow by more than $3.8 billion during the previous five quarters, which was referred to as 'one of the largest cases of false corporate bookkeeping yet'.[13] It was also speculated that WorldCom could face bankruptcy proceedings:

The [accounting] problem, discovered during an internal audit, throws into doubt the survival of WorldCom and MCI, the long-distance company it acquired in 1998. The company, which was already the subject of a federal investigation into its accounting practices, has been struggling to refinance $30 billion in debt. Its credit was relegated to junk-bond status last month, and even before last night's announcement, the stock price was down more than 94 percent so far this year. (*New York Times*, 26 June 2002: 1)

What was particularly disturbing to some commentators was that WorldCom had been able to manipulate its cash flows. To many people, cash and cash flow are objective concepts, which can be measured and verified more easily than 'profit' – which is often seen as more susceptible to subjective assumptions and judgements.

Even short-sellers, who had been profiting in the market from WorldCom's falling share price were surprised at the scale of the accounting disclosures. Short-sellers can profit from a company's declining share price by taking out a futures contract with an obligation to sell shares in the future but with the price fixed at the current market price. One short-seller was quoted as saying that investors cheered WorldCom's acquisition binge when its stock was rising and paid little attention to how the company generated its profits. That attitude encouraged the company to stretch accounting rules and take ever-bigger risks in an effort to keep its stock rising, and 'the executives, the money managers, the auditors, the CFOs, the CEOs, the ones that got ahead were the most reckless, the least ethical'.[14]

WORLDCOM AND SALOMON SMITH BARNEY

As WorldCom's share price continued to decline in 2002, it became apparent that the company's employees were particularly hard-hit through the system of employee stock options. For instance, many employees who wanted to exercise their options and then sell the shares came across obstacles. In 1997 WorldCom gave Salomon Smith Barney the exclusive right to administer the stock option plan. There were reports of complaints by employees that the Salomon Smith Barney brokers pushed employees to exercise their options but hold on to the shares by taking out loans negotiated by Salomon. This meant that employees were at risk if WorldCom shares declined. Also, the brokers earned large fees for recommending this strategy.[15]

On 27 June 2002, a Congressional committee issued subpoenas to John Sidgmore, Bernard Ebbers and Scott Sullivan. The congressional committee also issued a subpoena to Jack Grubman, the telecommunications analyst at Salomon Smith Barney. Jack Grubman was regarded as a star analyst of quoted companies in the telecommunications industry. He joined Salomon Smith Barney in 1994 and became friendly with Ebbers. He was an enthusiastic supporter of WorldCom and even when WorldCom's stock was falling after 1999, Grubman continued to rate the company's stock as a 'buy'.[16]

In May 2004, Citigroup (which controlled Salomon Smith Barney) announced that it would pay $2.65 billion to settle Worldcom investor lawsuits. Of the settlement, $1.19 billion went to investors who had bought stock in WorldCom between April 1999 and June 2002. The lawsuit had alleged that Jack Grubman 'had deliberately painted too positive a picture of WorldCom's prospects before an accounting misstatement drove it into bankruptcy'.[17]

WORLDCOM'S BANKRUPTCY

On 26 June 2002, the SEC formally charged the company with defrauding investors.[18] Then on 21 July 2002, WorldCom filed for Chapter 11 bankruptcy protection. There were concerns that because of the size of the bankruptcy there would be problems in the wider economy and ramifications for banks, suppliers and other telephone companies. At the time of the bankruptcy substantial numbers of employees were laid off and it was predicted that the shareholders would receive nothing for their shares. For employees who also held WorldCom's shares, the bankruptcy was a double blow.

It seemed that the political administration was becoming nervous at public reaction to WorldCom's bankruptcy, which followed soon after Enron's bankruptcy in December 2001. It was reported that public opinion polls were beginning to show signs of a crisis of confidence by the public in business and that a public backlash could partly explain the decision by the White House and Republicans to support corporate fraud and accounting legislation promoted by Senate Democrats.[19] On 30 July 2002, President G.W. Bush signed into law the Sarbanes–Oxley Act of 2002 which would initiate radical corporate reforms.

In August 2002 WorldCom revealed that it had found another $3.3 billion in accounting irregularities[20] and on 10 September 2002 Sidgmore resigned as WorldCom CEO. On 16 December 2002, a compensation plan for the new chief executive of WorldCom, Michael Capellas, was agreed by two federal judges. The compensation package would guarantee Capellas $20 million in cash and stock over the following three years.[21] Capellas was a former president of Hewlett Packard and it was known that Microsoft had wanted him to become number three executive of Microsoft after Bill Gates, chairman, and Steve Ballmer, chief executive. Hence the justification for the substantial compensation package offered to Capellas.

DISCUSSION

Mississippi was not one of the wealthiest states in the USA and the fact that WorldCom was based in the state was a source of pride to many Mississippians. While WorldCom was successfully growing, it provided employment and a source of wealth to the state. But many who lived in the state and many of WorldCom's employees bought shares in the company and were badly let down when the share price fell to seven cents in July 2002. This compared with a share price of $62 three years earlier. But while WorldCom was doing well, there is little doubt that it contributed to economic development in Mississippi.

WorldCom represents a fascinating case study since it encompasses a story of massive wealth accumulation based on the telecommunications and internet boom of the 1990s. If the telecommunications and merger boom of the 1990s had not ended so suddenly, there is some justification for believing that WorldCom might have weathered the storm and carried on. As WorldCom's business declined in 2001 and 2002, Sullivan shifted some expenses from the profit-and-loss account to the balance sheet, thereby showing improved earnings. It seemed that this was a desperate measure, perhaps seen by Sullivan as a temporary measure, to try to prevent or delay WorldCom's bankruptcy.

There is some evidence that Bernie Ebbers was a charismatic figure. Ebbers and Sullivan held the most important posts at WorldCom and they appeared able to dominate the board of directors. WorldCom's bankruptcy caused a severe loss of confidence in US business, especially since it came so soon after Enron's bankruptcy in December 2001. Is it possible for UK business to argue that such collapses are unlikely to occur in the UK? In other words, is the present state of corporate governance in the UK sufficiently robust to prevent a UK version of WorldCom?

According to the President of the Institute of Chartered Accountants in England and Wales in 2002:

> There is no systemic failure in this country in financial reporting, auditing or corporate governance. (Peter Wyman, *Accountancy*, July 2002: 124)

But Beth Holmes – in her article 'WorldCom: could it happen here?' (*Accountancy*, August 2002: 18–19) – makes a number of interesting comments. She argues that Peter Wyman is complacent in arguing that scandals such as Enron and WorldCom are unlikely to happen in the UK. Perhaps the UK has simply been lucky in avoiding such major scandals. After all, Maxwell, Polly Peck and BCCI all occurred in the UK over a decade ago and it could be argued that similar episodes could happen again because little radical change has taken place in UK corporate governance in recent years.

There is little doubt that employees and shareholders lost out as a result of WorldCom's bankruptcy. Creditors were also disadvantaged. One might also think that the banks that made large loans to WorldCom would also have suffered. Interestingly, Partnoy argues that the banks who lent to WorldCom were effectively insured against the bankruptcy because they had used credit derivatives to hedge their lending risk:

> Banks had done an estimated $10 billion of credit default swaps related to WorldCom. That meant that even though banks still held loans to WorldCom and were owed money in WorldCom's bankruptcy proceedings, they had sold the risk with those loans to someone else. The banks didn't have to worry about WorldCom's bankruptcy, because whatever they lost on WorldCom's loans they made up for with credit default swaps. Whatever happened, they were hedged. (Partnoy, 2004: 375–6)

By the end of 2002 it was hoped that, with the appointment of Capellas and a new management team, WorldCom would be able to re-establish itself. The company emerged from bankruptcy in May 2004 and the name 'WorldCom' has now been dropped in favour of MCI. There have been several prestigious appointments to the board in order to enhance the company's credibility. For instance, Nicholas Katzenbach (a former US Attorney General) was appointed chairman of MCI and Dennis Beresford (former chairman of the Financial Accounting Standards Board) was appointed a director. Although MCI was reporting losses by the end of 2004, there were expectations that the company had a reasonable chance of operating profitably.

Table 8.1 WorldCom: key events

1983	LDDS (Long Distance Discount Services) created
1985	Bernie Ebbers appointed chief executive officer of LDDS
1992	Scott Sullivan joins LDDS
1994	Scott Sullivan promoted to chief financial officer
1995	LDDS changes name to WorldCom
1998	WorldCom completes takeover of MCI
1999	WorldCom begins to reclassify some operating expenses as capital expenditure
2000	WorldCom shareholders approve takeover of Sprint, but regulators block deal
2001	Internal auditors find overpayments on sales commissions
March 2002	Public learns that WorldCom has loaned Ebbers $341 million
April 2002	Ebbers resigns as CEO; Sidgmore takes over
June 2002	Cynthia Cooper reports to WorldCom audit committee on capital expenditure accounting (13 June); Sullivan is dismissed as CFO (24 June); WorldCom reports cash flows overstated by $3.8 billion (26 June)
July 2002	WorldCom files for bankruptcy (21 July); Sarbanes-Oxley Act becomes law (30 July)
August 2002	WorldCom reports additional $3.3 billion in accounting irregularities
September 2002	Sidgmore resigns as CEO
December 2002	Federal judges approve compensation package for new CEO, Michael Capellas
March 2004	Sullivan pleads guilty to fraud and conspiracy and agrees to testify against Ebbers, who faces similar charges
May 2004	WorldCom emerges from bankruptcy and is renamed MCI

Discussion questions

1   Is it possible that the UK quoted company sector could experience its own version of WorldCom?
2   Should short-sellers be described as 'stakeholders'?
3   Identify the stakeholders who lost out when WorldCom filed for bankruptcy and describe the extent of their losses.
4   Identify the main lessons that can be learned from WorldCom's bankruptcy.
5   To what extent can ethics be considered part of the solution to prevent future bankruptcies such as WorldCom?

REFERENCES

Holmes, B. (2002) 'WorldCom: could it happen here?', *Accountancy*, August: 18–19.
Jeter, L.W. (2003) *Disconnected: Deceit and Betrayal at WorldCom.* New Jersey: Wiley.
Partnoy, F. (2004) *Infectious Greed: How Deceit and Risk Corrupted the Financial Markets.* London: Profile Books.

NOTES

1   *Financial Times*, 4 March 2004: 28.
2   See, for instance, Jeter, 2003: 54.
3   A particular feature of the 'pooling of interests' method of group accounting is that goodwill is not created and the effect on reported profits can be more favourable than under the acquisition method of group accounting.
4   *New York Times*, 11 November 1997: 1.
5   Jeter, 2003: 98.
6   Jeter, 2003: 91.
7   Jeter, 2003: 118.
8   *San Francisco Chronicle*, 8 March 2002: B1.
9   See Jeter, 2003: 140–1.
10   Jeter, 2003: 151.
11   Jeter, 2003: 168.
12   Jeter, 2003: 173–4.
13   *New York Times*, 26 June 2002: 1.
14   *New York Times*, 26 June 2002: 1.
15   *New York Times*, 31 March 2002: 1.
16   Jeter, 2003: 63.
17   *Financial Times*, 11 May 2004: 21.
18   *Washington Post*, 28 June 2002: E1.
19   *New York Times*, 2 August 2002: 1.
20   *New York Daily News*, 11 September 2002: 23.
21   *New York Times*, 17 December 2002: 10.

Parmalat

The financial problems of Parmalat first came to the public's attention in November 2003, when it became clear that the group was struggling to meet its cash commitments; on 8 December 2003, Parmalat was unable to make a bond repayment of €150 million. This quickly led to a sharp fall in the share price in December 2003, when share dealing was suspended, and the group suffered a dramatic financial collapse.

By August 2004, the government-appointed administrator, Enrico Bondi, had calculated that Parmalat's debts amounted to €14.5 billion and the creditors were likely to receive only a fraction of that amount, probably less than 10 per cent. Up to November 2003, Parmalat had been an apparently successful Italian multinational company, with its shares quoted on the Milan stock exchange. In the decade to 2003, Parmalat had experienced remarkable growth, with sales rising from €845m in 1992 to €7,590m in 2002 (see Figure 4). In 2002 over 60 per cent of these sales took place outside Europe.

In its Statement of Results and Strategies for the six months to 30 June 2003, the Parmalat Group describes itself as a food group with a focus on milk, dairy products and beverages. There had been remarkable growth in the 1990s, but by 2002 sales revenues seemed to be levelling off. Parmalat was perhaps seen to be a rather unexciting company, not subject to the same kinds of risk as other multinationals, for instance those in technology, media and telecommunications (TMT), still less the types of risk associated with financial trades in options and futures, which led to the downfall of Barings Bank in 1995. This view of a stable organization was reinforced by Calisto Tanzi, chairman and chief executive, who argued that Parmalat was committed to maintaining its global leadership in liquid milk. He also considered that Parmalat's phase of rapid expansion had been substantially completed, and from 2003 onwards the focus was to be on consolidation and maximizing value (see Parmalat Group: Message from the Chairman).

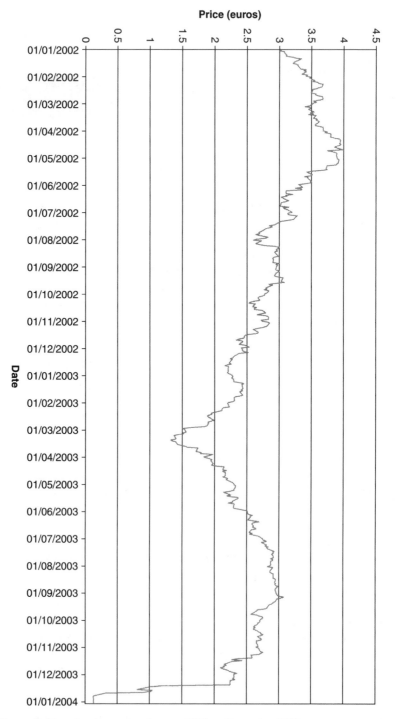

Figure 3 Parmalat share price, January 2002 to December 2003

Source: Datastream

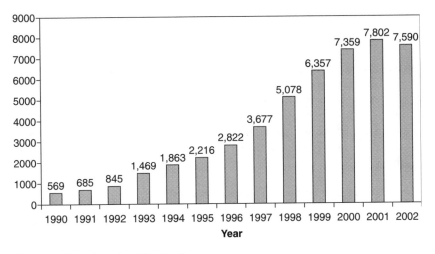

Figure 4 Parmalat sales (€ million)

Source: Parmlat Group Statement of Results and Strategies for six months to 30 June 2003

Parmalat Group: Message from the Chairman

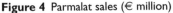

- Parmalat is a food group with a focus on milk, dairy products and beverages
- Parmalat is committed to continue to be the most innovative company in the market
- Parmalat is committed to deliver the best quality products to its consumers
- Parmalat is committed to expand its core brands Parmalat and Santàl
- Parmalat is committed to its consumers' satisfaction
- Parmalat is committed to providing attractive returns to its shareholders
- Parmalat is committed to its people
- Parmalat is committed to retain its global leadership in liquid milk
- Parmalat considers that the phase of rapid expansion is substantially completed. The focus is now on consolidation, maximizing value of the expansion

Source: Parmalat Group Statement of Results and Strategies for six months to 30 June 2003

GROUP FINANCIAL STATEMENTS

It is instructive to consider some of the financial statements produced by Parmalat in the months before it collapsed, although it needs to be remembered that both sales and assets had been fraudulently inflated by the management. Nevertheless, the profile of sales over the ten years before the group became bankrupt did show that in the three years from 2000 to 2002 they were beginning to level off. One normally expects companies to face cash flow problems while they are expanding, but not when they are stationary or even contracting.

Table 9.1 provides some key financial figures from Parmalat's consolidated accounts for the year ended 31 December 2002. One needs to remember that these are figures which were provided for public consumption. They do seem to indicate that the management was reaching the limits of creativity in accounting. With hindsight, it is questionable how turnover and earnings could fall by 3.3 per cent and 9.8 per cent respectively, but earnings per share could increase by 14.2 per cent. No doubt the latter figure justified holding the dividend at the same level as the previous year, which implied a cash outflow of €16.1m which the group could ill afford. Note that as the majority of shares in Parmalat were held by the Tanzi family, the major part of the dividend would have been paid to them.

Table 9.1 Parmalat: key financial figures (€ millions)

	2002	2001	change
turnover	7,590	7,802	−3.3%
EBITDA (1)	931	951	−2.1%
earnings before interest and tax	613	597	+2.7%
pre-tax earnings	373	414	−9.8%
net earnings for the year	252	218	+2.7%
earnings per share	0.313	0.274	+14.2%
dividend	16.1	15.9	+1.3%
dividend per share	0.020	0.020	
total shareholders' equity	2,250	2,835	−21.6%
net financial debt	1,862	1,956	−4.8%
gearing ratio (2)	45.3%	40.8%	

Notes:
[1] Earnings before interest, tax, depreciation and amortization
[2] Gearing ratio defined as debt/(debt + equity)

Source: Based on data published in Parmalat Group consolidated financial statements for year ended 31 December 2002 and Parmalat Group Statement of Results and Strategies for six months to 30 June 2003

Financial statements for the six months to 30 June 2003 also attempted to put over an impression of stability and the organization shifting direction as it coped with the problems arising from stabilization rather than expansion. The Parmalat Group Statement of Results and Strategies for the six months to 30 June 2003 indicated the group's financial strategies. Parmalat intended to gradually reduce its levels of debt by making appropriate use of its free cash flow:

- The overall strategy is to continue in a policy of lengthening maturities at competitive rates
- No new issues of equity linked, including convertible bonds
- Group's free cash flow will be directed to debt reduction
- The Group has maturities of Euro 3bn in the next three years. Euro 2bn will be refinanced. Euro 1bn will be reimbursed with its own resources

With hindsight, the group's intention to repay €1bn in debt over the following three years from internally generated resources had no credible foundation.

Finally, credit ratings from Standard and Poor's issued in August 2003 and September 2003, which were reproduced in Parmalat's interim financial statements, are broadly supportive of the group (although it needs to be remembered that Standard and Poor's were basing their analysis on fraudulently prepared information). Standard and Poor's report dated 19 August 2003 said in part:

> the ratings on leading global fluid milk processor Parmalat Finanziaria SpA and its operating subsidiary, Parmalat SpA, reflect the group's dominant domestic position in Italy, substantial geographical and product diversity, and core focus on branded and higher value-added categories which mitigate the commodity features of fluid milk. These positive factors are tempered by the group's moderate financial management and profile. At Dec. 31, 2002, Parmalat had gross debt of Euro 5.4 billion ($8.1 billion).

Their report of 15 September 2003 was quoted as saying:

> the stable outlook rests on Parmalat maintaining its solid operating performance as well as an adequate financial profile – in particular Funds from Operations (FFO) to Net Debt of at least 20 per cent – even when factoring in the likely buyout of minority shareholders in its Brazilian business. The group has commitments to buy out these minority shareholders for almost $400 million towards the end of 2003. The outlook also assumes that Parmalat gradually improves its financial management.

Investors reading the interim financial statements could be forgiven for accepting the apparent health of the company, given that it was described as having a 'dominant domestic position in Italy'. The only criticism comes in a description of the group's moderate financial management and profile, and a need for Parmalat to improve its financial management.

GROUP STRUCTURE

The name Parmalat was coined from Parma, the northern Italian town where the company was based, and *latte*, the Italian for milk. By 2003 Parmalat was a worldwide operation, most of the group sales taking place in Europe (nearly 40 per cent) and about one-third in North and Central America. Nearly 20 per cent of group sales were in South America. Finally, the rest of the world accounted for about 10 per cent of group sales, mainly in Australia, China and some countries in Southern Africa. Until 2003, Parmalat had been regarded as a successful business.

It had been founded in 1962 by Calisto Tanzi, when he was 22 years old. Tanzi had developed his family's local food business and introduced sales of carton milk. The company then broadened into other markets in the foodstuffs industry. By the 1970s Parmalat was making sales in other European countries; the 1980s and 1990s saw its expansion into North and South America. The extent of its apparent success can be judged by the fact that in 1990 the company purchased Parma Football Club, which was run by Stefano Tanzi, son of the founder, Calisto Tanzi. Substantial injections of resources allowed Parma Football Club to become one of the strongest teams in the Italian football league.

Calisto Tanzi was chairman and chief executive of Parmalat, and his son Stefano Tanzi was chairman of AC Parma. A daughter, Francesca Tanzi, was a director of subsidiary Parmatour, which was involved in the travel and leisure industry. It appeared that substantial financial resources were diverted from Parmalat to Parmatour, one report suggesting that nearly £350m was siphoned off from Parmalat to fund Parmatour (Hanney, 2004: 3). Calisto Tanzi himself was thought keen to acquire the trappings of status associated with substantial wealth and had even tried to emulate Silvio Berlusconi, the Italian prime minister and media magnate, by purchasing a television station for the Parmalat group.

It has been suggested[1] that part of the problem was that Parmalat was a family-owned business and its operations were opaque, even though it had had a listing on the Milan stock exchange since 1987. Parmalat's financial problems can be traced back a number of years before 2003, yet the group had apparently managed to convince banks, investors, financial regulators and the public that it was a soundly run company. However, as events unfolded in the months following the December 2003 collapse, it emerged that concerns were being expressed several months before the collapse.

One of the features of the Parmalat Group was its complicated organizational structure, including over 170 subsidiaries. Substantial funds were moved between these subsidiaries, some of which were registered in the Cayman Islands, a tax haven, and this increased the difficulty of monitoring cash flows and assets. For instance, Bonlat, a subsidiary registered in the Cayman Islands, was supposed to hold €3.95bn in liquid assets in a Bank of America account in New York. But in December 2003 it transpired that Bonlat had provided false documentation about the asset to its auditor, Grant Thornton.

On 15 December 2003, Calisto Tanzi resigned as chairman and chief executive of Parmalat. The following day Enrico Bondi – appointed by the Italian government as an administrator to Parmalat – assumed responsibility for managing the affairs of the group. In attempting to put Parmalat back on a sound financial basis, it seems that he soon came to the view that the banks who had provided loan finance to Parmalat should also share part of the blame for the group's collapse.

Early on in the investigation, prosecutors were helped by a Parmalat employee who had disobeyed instructions to destroy sensitive documents and had handed over a computer and disks to investigators. As the investigation got under way, it was found that Parmalat had established a network of subsidiaries through which it had been able to channel substantial amounts of financial resources. It proved difficult for the administrator to establish the full extent of these offshore transactions. In December 2003, a number of Parmalat executives were arrested and investigating magistrates began to piece together a picture of events.

At the time of his arrest, Calisto Tanzi claimed that any funds removed from the company while he was in charge were relatively small. But he subsequently admitted that he had channelled €500m to the travel company Parmatour. In addition, he at first denied that any falsification of accounts had occurred, but he soon admitted knowledge of the falsification. According to one report, Calisto Tanzi told magistrates that he did not understand very much about balance sheets. 'I realized certain needs of my companies and I asked my managers to fix things. Then they would inform me in the broadest sense'.[2]

When questioned about the falsification of the Bank of America account, Calisto Tanzi claimed that he only became aware of this in November 2003, when he was informed by Fausto Tonna and Luciano del Soldato, both high-ranking financial officers in Parmalat. However, Tonna was not keen to accept the blame for these events and challenged Calisto Tanzi's version of events. According to Tonna, Tanzi was well aware of the group's financial difficulties and, indeed, it was Tanzi's idea to try to disguise them. Tanzi had also requested Tonna not to inform the board of directors about the financial irregularities. Another director, Luciano del Soldato, when interrogated, claimed that a decision to destroy documents relating to the Bonlat subsidiary in the Cayman Islands was made jointly by Fausto Tonna and Calisto Tanzi. Fausto Tonna also attempted to implicate the Italian firm of Grant Thornton SpA, saying that they had actually been involved in setting up the offshore companies in the Caribbean, which allowed Tanzi to manipulate funds and hide the group's true financial position.

It was becoming clear that no single high-ranking officer in Parmalat was prepared to accept full responsibility for what had happened, and that the underlying causes had preceded the December 2003 financial collapse by several years. Another executive, Giovanni Bonici, head of Parmalat's Venezuelan operations, when questioned by magistrates claimed that he had simply been following senior management directives and had sometimes been sent only the last page of contracts for his signature.

By August 2004, Enrico Bondi had decided to extend his legal actions against some of the banks who had assisted Parmalat in issuing bonds and loans. It was revealed that the administrator was pursuing Deutsche Bank, UBS and Citigroup for substantial compensation. Enrico Bondi and Italian prosecutors believed that Deutsche Bank, Bank of America, Citigroup, UBS and some other financial institutions had been aware of Parmalat's weak financial position before it finally collapsed in December 2003. However, the banks had continued to facilitate finance for the group, receiving large fees in return. This was disputed by the banks, claiming instead that they were also exposed to losses on Parmalat's loans.

THE REGULATORS AND THE INVESTORS

In February 2003 Parmalat announced that it intended to make a bond issue of €300m, although it was unable to justify the need for the cash. A bond issue at that time seemed curious since the group claimed to have more than €3bn in cash. Critical comments from the investment community[3] resulted in the share price of Parmalat falling, and the bond issue was abandoned. The response of Parmalat to this criticism was to go to the Italian financial regulator, Consob, and to ask it to investigate the financial institutions who had expressed criticism of Parmalat's finances. No doubt the intention of Parmalat's management was to attempt to silence its critics. Given the state of the company's finances, Parmalat could only survive by issuing yet more debt and in order to do this it needed the confidence of the banks and investors. But this was not helped by the fact that in 2003 fund managers were apparently complaining about the lack of transparency and the group's inability to service and pay back debts (Quick, 2004: 29).

Nevertheless, by July 2003 Consob was pressing Parmalat for more detailed information about its finances. Eventually, in November 2003, Parmalat claimed to Consob that it intended to liquidate by 27 November an investment of nearly €500m held in Epicurum, an obscure investment fund in the Cayman Islands. In November 2003, as concerns about the liquidity and finances of Parmalat began to leak out to the market, investors began to sell stock, which caused the share price to decline. However, one equities analyst at Citigroup somewhat surprisingly changed his rating in the middle of November from 'hold' to 'buy' which would have been seen as a positive signal to the market.

But, as the days passed, it became apparent that Parmalat was unable to realize the investment by the due date. The Cayman Islands Monetary Authority, which was responsible for regulating such activities, later claimed that Epicurum was not registered and therefore not monitored since it had less than 15 investors. News of the non-existence of the Epicurum funds was then followed by the revelation that €3.95bn in cash supposedly held in a Bank of America account did not exist either.

PARMALAT'S FINANCIAL ADVISERS

A main part of the investigation into Parmalat has centred around the activities of Gian Paolo Zini. He was the founder of the legal firm Zini &

Associates, which gave legal advice to Parmalat over a number of years. One of the features of corporate collapses, where the management is keen to cover its tracks, is the phenomenon of shredding vital evidence that could prove incriminating in a court of law. So it was perhaps not surprising that there were reports that, as the events at Parmalat unfolded, some key staff were busy at Zini & Associates removing or destroying computer files and documents.

The New York offices of Zini & Associates were raided by the Manhattan District Attorney on 31 December 2003, but there were fears that important documents had already been removed:

> According to several employees of Zini & Associates in New York . . . there was good reason to worry that crucial documents had been removed . . . Cartons of documents were being removed by the trolley-load in the weeks before the raid, the employees say . . . Among the files to which employees were unable to gain access were those related to Bonlat, the Parmalat subsidiary based in the Cayman islands which falsely claimed to have €3.95bn in a Bank of America account at the end of 2002. No such account existed, and Parmalat executives in Italy have since admitted destroying Bonlat files there. (*Financial Times*, 5 February 2004: 27)

It appeared that a main reason for the existence of Zini & Associates was to provide legal services to Parmalat, for instance, helping with issues of bonds to international investors. In addition the law firm filed complaints – in the USA in May 2003, with the SEC and Nasdaq – that hedge funds were manipulating Parmalat stock. Zini & Associates had also been instrumental in making similar complaints in March 2003 to Consob, the Italian regulator.

Zini & Associates had been responsible for creating Epicurum, the Cayman Islands-based fund that supposedly held almost €500m of Parmalat's cash. Towards the end of November 2003, as questions were increasingly being asked by investors about the fund, neither Epicurum nor its officers could be reached. A website created for Epicurum by Zini & Associates reportedly stated it was 'under construction':

> In preliminary hearings (in January 2004) seeking his exit from jail, Mr Zini claimed he knew nothing of Parmalat's accounting 'hole' and was simply executing orders. He denied accusations from a senior Parmalat accountant that he advised the accountant to destroy evidence, according to transcripts of the interrogations. According to investigating magistrates, Fausto Tonna, Parmalat's long-time chief financial officer, accused Mr Zini of being at the centre of Parmalat's financial schemes. After that, the judges rejected Mr Zini's arguments and he remains incarcerated in Parma. (*Financial Times*, 5 February 2004: 27)

THE AUDITORS

The auditing side of Parmalat was quite complex. Deloitte, one of the world's largest auditing firms, acted as the chief auditor for Parmalat. Previously, Grant Thornton had been the chief auditor but had handed over to Deloitte in 1999 because of an Italian company law requirement that auditors need to change every eight years. However, Deloitte had retained Grant Thornton SpA to audit some subsidiaries and it was Grant Thornton SpA who came in for the strongest criticism. In fact, shortly after news of the scandal first broke, two of the senior partners of Grant Thornton SpA, Maurizio Bianchi and Lorenza Penca, were arrested.

Grant Thornton International ranks as a medium-sized accounting organization on the global scene. However, although it is a global name, in practice it operates as a network of firms and the Italian firm, Grant Thornton SpA, was legally independent from firms in other countries with the label Grant Thornton (Haythornthwaite, 2004). Most large auditing firms that operate internationally are essentially networks of independent national firms, rather than one global firm. In fact, it would be more accurate to speak of global accounting 'brands' rather than firms. A network of independent national firms has the advantage that, if there are problems with one particular national firm, then the remainder of the network can quickly move to distance itself from the 'problem firm'. The disadvantage is that clients may not realize that their national auditor is legally independent from the remainder of the network.

Grant Thornton International quickly realized the potential harm to its global brand and in January 2004 dropped the Italian practice from Grant Thornton International. No doubt, Grant Thornton International – in other words, the remaining firms in the network – were aware of the damage that could be done to their reputation and business in other countries, in the light of what had happened to Arthur Andersen, which had been sucked under with Enron and WorldCom. Grant Thornton's US business contacted its clients to emphasize that it had no role in the audit of Parmalat.

Deloitte itself, even though it was the chief auditor, appeared to come in for less criticism than Grant Thornton. Giuseppe Rovelli, on behalf of Deloitte Italy, signed the auditor's report on the consolidated financial statements for 2002. Unlike Grant Thornton International, Deloitte did not move to drop the Italian firm from its international network. The audit report gives a positive opinion on the Parmalat Group and concludes:

> In our opinion, the consolidated financial statements present fairly the financial position of the Group as of December 31, 2002, and the results of its operations for the year then ended, and comply with the principles which regulate the preparation of consolidated financial statements in Italy.

Any shareholder or other interested party, reading such a statement, would have little reason to suspect that there was much amiss with the affairs of Parmalat. However, earlier in the audit report, it was stated that:

> The financial statements of certain subsidiary companies representing 49 per cent of consolidated total assets and 30 per cent of consolidated revenues respectively have been examined by other auditors who provided us with copies of their reports. Our opinion, expressed in this report, as regards the figures relating to such companies included in the consolidation, is also based on the work carried out by these other auditors. We believe that our audit provides a reasonable basis for our opinion.

With hindsight, it has been suggested that relying on other firms to carry out such a large proportion of the audit may not have been wise. 'One senior accountant at another "big four" firm said he would be uneasy about such a high degree of reliance on other audit firms, and would exercise increased levels of oversight in such circumstances'.[4] Considering the size of the Bank of America account, it was curious that Grant Thornton SpA did not take additional steps to check on the existence of the account or even send an employee to New York to verify it.

As it turned out, reliance on the audit work of Grant Thornton SpA was one of the reasons why news of Parmalat's true state of affairs did not reach the markets more quickly. Was Grant Thornton damaged by the Parmalat scandal? By March 2004, there was evidence[5] that Grant Thornton International was losing clients at a faster rate than it was picking up new ones. In response, the firm claimed that this was partly because it had taken the decision to resign from the audit of companies where Grant Thornton perceived that the level of risk was unacceptably high, due to questionable accounting methods.

By April 2004, Deloitte Italy was increasingly being drawn into the financial scandal. One report[6] indicated that Deloitte Italy had signed off the 2001 consolidated accounts of Parmalat even though no audit report had been received for the Brazilian subsidiary, one of the group's largest operations. In fact, Deloitte Brazil had apparently raised serious questions on the 2001 accounts but the Brazilian auditor – who had requested fuller information from the Italian parent company – was taken off the Parmalat account. Some of Parmalat's top executives also claimed that the Deloitte Italy auditors were aware of account '999', which showed a debit of over €8bn at the end of 2002. But Gianfranco Bocchi, a Parmalat accountant, claimed that its purpose was essentially to hide the faked revenues and assets which had accumulated over a number of years, and this had been explained in some detail to the Deloitte Italy auditors.

DISCUSSION

A matter of concern must be the issue of whether large accounting firms are able to monitor effectively the affairs of large multinational companies such as Parmalat. Some audit firms rely on the work of other audit firms in carrying out the overall audit. In the case of Parmalat, the chief auditor, Deloitte, relied on audit work carried out by Grant Thornton. As it turned out, Grant Thornton SpA had relied on false documentation provided by the management of Parmalat. Therefore, there are necessarily risks when one audit firm is forced to rely on the work of another audit firm. This would seem to suggest that the audit of the parent company and all the subsidiaries in a multinational should be carried out by a single audit firm. The argument would be that in a single audit firm one would expect audit procedures to be carried out consistently across all countries.

However, the notion of a global audit firm is somewhat removed from reality in the modern world. In effect the global firms are better described as global networks, or even global brands, and the national partnerships that make up these global brands are effectively independent of each other. As Haythornthwaite (2004: 33) states 'The danger of appearing more global is that, regardless of legal independence, the whole network's reputation is at stake when one member firm gets into trouble. David McDonnell, [chief executive officer] of Grant Thornton International, refused to speak to *Accountancy*, but has reportedly admitted that the Parmalat scandal will inevitably damage Grant Thornton's international name'.

So the large audit firms face a dilemma. On the one hand, their clients would like the security associated with being audited by one of the largest audit firms, and the prestige associated with a large audit firm's name on the audit report. On the other hand, the audit firms themselves need to make it clear that they function as a network of independent national partnerships, if they are to minimize the damage to the remainder of the network when something goes wrong in a particular country. In the case of Grant Thornton International, the Italian partnership was quickly dropped from the international network soon after news of financial problems became public knowledge.

Table 9.2 Parmalat: key events

1962	Parmalat founded by Calisto Tanzi
1987	Parmalat shares listed on Milan stock exchange
February 2003	Parmalat announces intention to make a bond issue of €300 million; critical comments from the investment community and a falling share price lead to the bond issue being abandoned
July 2003	Consob presses Parmalat for more information about its finances
November 2003	Market rumours express concern at state of Parmalat's liquidity
December 2003	Parmalat fails to make €150 million bond repayment; Calisto Tanzi resigns as chairman and chief executive; Parmalat is placed into administration; share dealing is suspended
August 2004	Enrico Bondi, administrator for Parmalat, calculates that debts total €14.5 billion and creditors are likely to receive less than 10%

Discussion questions

1 How would you attempt to apportion blame amongst the various parties involved in the financial collapse at Parmalat?
2 It has been argued that the largest audit firms are no longer global firms as such but rather global 'brands' or 'networks'. Discuss whether this is an appropriate description and, if appropriate, what the likely consequences could be.
3 Were there any missed opportunities which might have allowed the financial affairs of Parmalat to be disclosed to the public before December 2003?
4 What mechanisms or procedures would you suggest could be put in place in an attempt to avoid a repetition of the Parmalat scandal?
5 Discuss the potential conflicts of interest that can arise when financial institutions are involved in raising finance for large companies and at the same time offering investment advice to clients and the public.

REFERENCES

Hanney, B. (2004) 'The men in the frame', *Accountancy*, February: 30.
Haythornthwaite, A. (2004) 'Myth, reality and the global firm', *Accountancy*, February: 32–3.
Quick, C. (2004) 'The milk giant that turned sour', *Accountancy*, February: 28–9.

NOTES

1 *Financial Times*, 22 December 2003: 18.
2 *Financial Times*, 3 January 2004: M4.
3 *Financial Times*, 9 January 2004: 15
4 *Financial Times*, 3 January 2004: M4.
5 *Financial Times*, 18 March 2004: 45.
6 *Financial Times*, 10 April 2004: 1.

Eurotunnel[1]

TEN

This chapter examines, using a principal–agent framework, the case of Eurotunnel, which operates the Channel Tunnel and provides a permanent rail link between the UK and France. The main services consist of passenger and freight shuttles, as well as through passenger trains (Eurostar) and freight trains. Eurotunnel has recently widened its operations to encompass retailing (as a competitor to ferry operators), property development and even telecommunications.

Plans for a fixed link between the UK and France go back some 200 years. The earliest feasible plan is reckoned to have been devised by Albert Mathieu in 1802.[2] Mathieu envisaged twin bored tunnels between Cap Gris Nez near Calais and Eastwell Bay near Folkestone, surprisingly close in design and location to the present Eurotunnel. During the nineteenth century various schemes were proposed, many spurred on by the development of the railways. However, apart from obvious considerations such as construction cost, one of the stumbling blocks proved to be the issue of national defence and the question of the security of the UK from possible invasion. By the mid-1970s, it seemed that the issue of national security was no longer a major obstacle and that a collaborative project for a twin bored tunnel might actually go ahead. However, the plan was finally cancelled by the UK government in 1975, mainly on the grounds of rapidly escalating costs, disruption to the parliamentary timetable caused by two general elections in 1974, and environmental considerations (Holliday, Marcou and Vickerman, 1991).

By the 1980s the UK government had made it clear that it would support a fixed link only if public funding was not involved. In April 1985 the French and UK governments invited tenders for the construction and operation of a fixed link and, from a shortlist of four consortia, the two governments selected the Eurotunnel proposal in early 1986. In July 1987 the governments ratified a treaty to regulate the construction and operation of the system. The original concession (since extended) was signed in August 1987 and was for the construction and operation of a Channel Tunnel link until July 2042.

EUROTUNNEL IS FLOATED

In November 1987 an *Offer for Sale* – of 220m units at £3.50 each – raised £770m of equity and excavation began in December 1987. At first, expectations about the commercial viability of the project were generally high. The share price had fallen sharply after the November 1987 *Offer for Sale,* which was in fact undersubscribed, partly due to the October 1987 stock market crash. But by March 1988 the share price had almost recovered to the offer price. By the end of 1988 the share price was beginning to rise sharply until in June 1989 it reached a peak of £11.64, which prompted Alastair Morton, at that time Co-Chairman, to warn the following month that the share price was 'ahead of expectations'.[3] However, this proved to be a temporary period of optimism and by the end of 1989 the share price had suffered a steep fall. Nevertheless it remained above the offer price for some time, until late 1994 in fact. Thereafter, the share price entered a period of decline.

The period from December 1987 up to May 1994 involved construction work and in June 1994 commercial operations began. With the useful benefit of hindsight, it is clear that mistakes were made. For instance, by 1994 it was evident that the eventual construction cost would be almost double that predicted in 1987. Many of the original traffic and revenue projections proved over-optimistic. In April 2004 the chairman and chief executive of Eurotunnel were voted out of office by the shareholders and by the end of the month the share price[4] stood at 28p compared with the *Offer for Sale* price in November 1987 of £3.50. In addition, no dividends had been declared or paid over this period.

Fragmented share ownership and the agency problem

There were no significantly large shareholdings in Eurotunnel, and share ownership was fragmented throughout France and the UK. From a principal–agent perspective, when shareholdings are widely dispersed there is little incentive to monitor management. Monitoring is a public good and if one shareholder's monitoring leads to improved company performance then all shareholders benefit. Since monitoring is costly, shareholders free-ride in the hope that other shareholders will carry out the monitoring activities and the likely consequence is that little or no monitoring will actually take place. Large investors can reduce agency costs since they can exert influence over the agent and therefore do not need as many rights as small investors to protect their interests (see Shleifer and Vishny, 1997).

As discussed in Chapter 2, the agency problem is now seen as an important element of the contractual view of the firm. The analysis focuses on the impossibility of writing complete contracts and the complexities arising from incomplete contracts. Principals and agents tend to write incomplete contracts because it is difficult for people to think ahead and plan for all possible contingencies; it is not easy for the contracting parties to negotiate effectively; and it is difficult for plans to be written down in such a way that an outside authority, such as a court, will be able to interpret and enforce the contract. Therefore, it is not possible to resolve all potential conflicts between the agent and the principal so one view is that Eurotunnel's financial problems are partly attributable to the inherent problems associated with incomplete contracts.

CONSTRUCTION: DECEMBER 1987 TO MAY 1994

Although the November 1987 *Offer for Sale* showed relatively detailed projections of income and expenditure over the life of the Concession, a surprising omission was any phasing of capital expenditure during the construction period. Projected information on an annual basis over the construction period would be relevant in assisting potential investors in the *Offer for Sale* to monitor the size and implications of any cost over-runs, yet this information was not provided. The principals (shareholders) were in a weak position *vis-à-vis* the agent (management) in that no benchmark was available *ex-ante* against which to measure the growth of capital expenditure.

What is curious in the early years of the project is how the share price managed to rise so sharply. It reached a peak of £11.64 in June 1989, yet it is not clear what favourable information in the meantime could have been responsible for this major shift in market sentiment. Given that rights issues took place in November 1990 and May 1994, share prices in Figure 5 have been adjusted (downwards) in the earlier years to enable a fair comparison with share prices after 1994. Therefore the peak in June 1989 was equivalent to £7.92 when restated in terms of the current share price.

Delays in the construction programme carried four adverse implications for the eventual cost of the project: financing costs would accumulate to a larger extent; labour costs would increase; unforeseen problems in the works programme would require costly modifications to equipment; and there would be a delayed start to operations and therefore a delay in revenues coming on stream. Could the market have predicted at an early stage that all was not well with the progress of construction? Not from the 1988 accounts it appears. The 1988 annual report and accounts, which were published in April 1989, gave little indication that anything was amiss after the first year of construction.

However, the following year, the 1989 Directors' Report of Eurotunnel plc (published in April 1990) contained a much longer and more informative section. Amongst other aspects, it referred to the fact that in late 1988 relations between Eurotunnel and its contractor (TML) had been 'highly strained'. Clearly, problems with the progress of the project

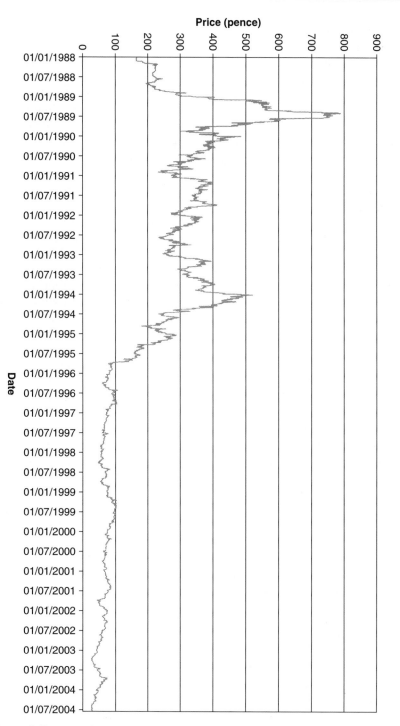

Figure 5 Eurotunnel share price, January 1988 to June 2004

Source: Datastream

had been appreciated *within* the company since late 1988, but this information did not reach the market until many months later.

Did the management of Eurotunnel have an obligation to make these matters known more widely at an earlier date? Presumably the management hoped that the problems were temporary. Publicizing these difficulties would only alarm the market and thereby endanger any future financing. On the other hand, an escalating share price carried with it the danger that new shareholders would be attracted to the project and invest at an inflated share price. These issues highlight the potential conflicts in an agency relationship where the agent could have an incentive to maintain the momentum of the project regardless of cost, whereas the principals were keen to minimize costs.

Anecdotal evidence indicates that a number of private investors were attracted to the project in 1988 and early 1989 and subsequently lost considerable sums of money.[5] Several years later they formed a vociferous shareholder association, Adacte, which attempted to take legal action against the directors. At that time, Adacte failed to gain any redress against the directors, an example perhaps of the difficulties faced by a fragmented share ownership in trying to exert its will over management. Some were undoubtedly naïve in their understanding of the workings of the stock market and in their belief that the French and UK governments would make good any shortfall. The *Financial Times* in 1997 quoted one French shareholder as saying, 'I didn't know what shares were. I thought they were safe like loans. I believed the French and British governments were more or less behind the project'.[6]

Given the inherent uncertainties attached to the project, especially in the early years, and the consequent share price volatility, share purchases represented a fairly speculative investment. If it is accepted that a major goal of the agent was to ensure that the project was ultimately completed (cost being a secondary consideration) then this goal would be assisted by optimistic public announcements. On the other hand, optimism on the part of the agent was inconsistent with the main objective of the principals (which was likely to be that of maximizing the net present value of their investment).

The construction problems facing Eurotunnel involved three technical areas: tunnelling, rolling stock and design changes.

Tunnelling

Tunnelling started more slowly than expected. The November 1987 *Offer for Sale* declared that 90 per cent of the undersea section was expected to be bored in the 'most favourable geological layer, consisting of chalk marl, which is virtually impermeable and generally considered ideal for tunnelling' (Eurotunnel, 1987: 20). The only significant area of difficult conditions was thought to be near the French coast, where specially designed tunnelling machines would be used. In fact, the ground conditions under the British side proved much worse than had been thought,[7] with salt water in the rock affecting the performance of the tunnel boring machines. This caused delays and required expensive modifications to the machinery.

In the November 1987 *Offer for Sale* it was stated that 'The contract provides financial incentives for the Contractor [TML] to complete the tunnels under budget and financial penalties if they are completed over budget or late. It also provides financial penalties if the Contractor completes the System late. This arrangement is designed to encourage the cost-effective completion of the System on time' (Eurotunnel, 1987: 21). It later transpired that TML's contribution to cost over-runs was limited to a relatively favourable 6 per cent, although a revised agreement later re-apportioned cost over-runs between Eurotunnel (70 per cent) and TML (30 per cent).[8]

Rolling stock

Unexpected increases in the cost of rolling stock occurred. In 1991 the Finance Director of Eurotunnel was quoted as saying 'In all honesty one now must say that the original rolling stock estimates were put together with insufficient awareness of the complexities of the one-off stock which we would need'.[9] Design changes were imposed by the Inter-Governmental Commission, established by the French and UK governments and responsible for granting Eurotunnel an operating licence. For example, the Commission required fire doors connecting the shuttle wagons to be widened by 10cm, an apparently minor requirement but one which necessitated substantial and costly re-engineering.[10]

Design changes

No cooling system had been envisaged in the original proposal. It later became evident that friction caused by the trains as well as heat generated by electrical equipment could raise the temperature inside the tunnel to 50°C. Eventually, an elaborate cooling system was installed, carrying chilled water through several hundred kilometres of piping. Also, the substantial air pressure created by trains travelling at up to 160kph (100mph) meant that all the tunnel components needed to be re-designed to new aerodynamic standards.

Although some differences between plan and outcome might have been foreseen at the time of writing the original prospectus, it is impossible to write a complete, precise and watertight contingent contract for each possible outcome. In the jargon of the transaction cost literature, the parties (principal and agent) engaged in a long-term, incomplete financial contract.

COMMERCIAL OPERATION: JUNE 1994 ONWARDS

Eurotunnel opened officially on 6 May 1994, 12 months later than had been predicted in the November 1987 *Offer for Sale*. The management took advantage of the publicity surrounding the official opening to make a further rights issue. The May 1994 rights issue was for 324m units @ £2.65 per unit and this largely accounts for the increase in shareholders' funds in that year. In 1994, equity (including share premium) increased by £909m. The main reason for the May 1994 rights issue was the realization that the financing of the heavy debt burden, together with the delay in commercial operations, meant that cash deficits would continue to build up until 1998, by which time it was predicted that operating cash flows would be sufficient to absorb the financing costs. Although by May 1994 most of the capital costs were established and understood, the projected revenues (and hence projected operating cash flows) were substantially over-optimistic. This would mean that the target of cash break-even in 1998 could not be met.

Despite the delays in commissioning the system and delays in obtaining the necessary systems acceptance certificates, by December 1994 the Eurotunnel system was virtually fully operational. During 1995 it became clear that Eurotunnel's actual revenues were seriously below target. On 14 September 1995 the management of Eurotunnel took the major step of suspending interest payments on its main (junior) debt. Junior debt formed the bulk of its total debt. This operation – referred to as 'standstill' – allowed Eurotunnel a breathing space in which the banks agreed not to pursue unpaid interest through legal channels, while Eurotunnel attempted to resolve its debt problems. The period of standstill was to last until 14 December 1997. The Chairmen's letter to the shareholders, dated 19 April 1996 and sent out with the 1995 accounts, cited three major factors likely to adversely affect future cash flows.

The first threat to Eurotunnel's cash flows was fierce competition, in other words reduced prices charged by ferry operators. Eurotunnel maintained that the ferry companies were able to charge fares below cost because the fares were subsidized by duty-free sales. The special duty-free regime, which tended to favour the ferry companies rather than Eurotunnel, was phased out by the European Union in mid-1999.

The second factor weakening cash flow was the failure of the railway companies to develop traffic according to their predictions. The actual figures for passengers and freight carried in 1995 were about one-third of the levels previously forecast.

The third problem for future cash flow was the increase in operating costs resulting from the complexity and shortcomings of the rolling stock specified and delivered by TML. Eurotunnel also cited the onerous requirements of the governments and the Intergovernmental Commission in terms of operational procedures.

During 1996, Eurotunnel's main preoccupation was with its debt problems and protracted negotiations with the banks. On top of these problems, on 18 November 1996 a serious fire occurred on a freight shuttle. This proved to be a significant setback at a time when commercial operations appeared to be progressing well. Total revenue in 1996 was up by 50 per cent compared to 1995, the first full year of operation. Repair works to the tunnel affected by the fire were not completed until May 1997 and this caused all services to be interrupted. The freight shuttle, which was the worst affected, was not able to operate for about seven months.

In May 1997 Eurotunnel issued its *Financial Restructuring Proposals*. The main objectives in restructuring the group's debt were to reduce the actual amount of debt and also reduce the cost of servicing the debt. These objectives were achieved in a number of ways, which resulted in an extremely complex set of financial arrangements. The restructuring proposals were approved by the shareholders in July 1997. Some members of Adacte, the shareholder action group, were outraged that the banks should be treated so 'favourably'. However, the general consensus at the time appears to have been that there was no other choice, and to agree with the management that without the necessary shareholder approval, 'there is no reasonable prospect of avoiding insolvency procedures in the UK and France. In such circumstances, Unitholders would be unlikely to receive any return on their investment' (Eurotunnel, 1997). At the same time as achieving agreement on the financial restructuring, Eurotunnel was able to obtain agreement from the French and UK governments to a substantial extension to the period of the concession, that is, from 2052 to 2086.[11]

EUROTUNNEL PROSPECTUS FORECASTS AND SHARE PRICE MOVEMENTS

In the early years of the project, the Eurotunnel management – and Alastair Morton in particular – were strongly criticized in the media and by some financial analysts for providing over-optimistic forecasts of the future revenues and financial prospects of Eurotunnel. Financial analyst Richard Hannah of UBS, a long-term critic of Eurotunnel's forecasts, was quoted as saying, 'had the investors originally known the degree of uncertainty in the prospectus, they probably never would have put the money in'.[12] In November 1997, the Lex column in the *Financial Times* referred to Eurotunnel's previous forecasts as having proved 'comically optimistic'.[13]

A summary of some important data contained in the prospectus forecasts is shown in Table 10.1. Note that the term 'prospectus' is used here to describe the November 1987 *Offer for Sale*, the Rights Issues of November 1990 and May 1994, and the May 1997 *Financial Restructuring Proposals*. The data in Table 10.1, which cover these four prospectus events, are fairly comparable since they all include estimates for inflation. The revenue estimates given in November 1987 and November 1990 are almost identical for first full year of operation (1994) and succeeding years. But it can readily be observed that the projected revenues were substantially over-estimated. Thus the November 1987 revenue estimate for first full year of operation (1994) was £762m, which was 151 per cent higher than actual revenue achieved in the first full year (1995) of operation (£304m). In some respects, the Eurotunnel project bears comparison with an earlier Anglo-French project, the Concorde. In both cases capital costs were severely understated and projected revenues were substantially overestimated.

Table 10.1 Eurotunnel prospectus forecasts, 1993–2003 (£m)

	November 1987	November 1990	May 1994	May 1997	actual revenue
1993	488	393	–	–	–
1994	762	764	137	–	82
1995	835	833	525	–	304
1996	908	904	737	–	483
1997	986	980	829	567	531
1998	1,072	1,070	901	649	666
1999	1,158	1,165	993	654	654
2000	1,254	1,258	1,056	572	600
2001	1,356	1,358	1,130	645	564
2002	1,466	1,464	1,205	699	581
2003	1,586	1,582	1,308	760	584

Source: Eurotunnel prospectuses, 1987 to 1997

The figures for profit before tax likewise proved to be substantially over-estimated. The higher than anticipated capital costs resulted in increased depreciation charges and increased interest charges because a major part of the capital overspend was financed by debt (rather than equity). Instead of £108m profit before tax estimated for the first full year of operation (as predicted at November 1987), there was a loss of £924m in the actual first full year of operation (1995).

The unexpected escalation in the construction costs and the low revenues together help to explain share price[14] movements over the period under study (Figure 5). The offer price in November 1987 was 350p. The share issue was undersubscribed and the share price fell to 250p. At its peak in June 1989 the share price reached £11.64p.

A striking feature of the share price profile is how volatility has generally decreased over time. From being a high-risk investment in December 1987 when shares were first traded publicly, Eurotunnel has become a much lower-risk 'utility'. The period of greatest volatility was from September 1988 to September 1989. It is quite possible that, if the concerns about construction progress had been better appreciated in the market, then the exceptionally high prices recorded in May and June 1989 would not have occurred.

The comment has often been made that 'one day someone will make a lot of money out of Eurotunnel'. For those investors fortunate enough to sell at or near the top of the 1988/9 share price 'bubble', that is already a reality. But if they bought at the peak and were still holding their shares by the end of April 2004 they would have lost over 95 per cent of the capital value of their investment, not to mention the opportunity cost of a zero return on their investment. Also badly hit have been the original investors who (assuming they were still holding their shares at the end of April 2004) have lost nearly 90 per cent of their investment. Once again the actual loss is even greater, given the opportunity cost of zero return on investment. In some cases the losses of original investors have been mitigated by the travel privileges attached to their investment, the extent of these privileges being dependent on the size of the original investment.

The November 1990 rights issue raised £570m and it is interesting to note that timing. It was useful for Eurotunnel because on 30 October contact had been made by a probe in the service tunnel between the French and UK sides and this generated useful positive publicity. The May 1994 Rights Issue, which raised £816m, also came shortly after some positive publicity, that surrounding the official opening ceremony on 6 May 1994.

From mid-1994 onwards the share price entered a period of sustained decline. But in October 1994 Sir Alastair Morton, ever the optimist, bought 5,000 units at £2.30 and heroically proclaimed 'I'll hold these new shares for at least a year and sell them when the holding shows me 50 per cent per annum growth'.[15] One year later, in mid-October 1995, the shares were standing at just over 80p, having lost about 70 per cent of their value over the preceding year. It is difficult to see how a co-chairman could get it so wrong.

On 14 September 1995, Eurotunnel announced that it was suspending interest payments on its main debt. Over the following week the share price dropped by 29 per cent. From then until the end of April 2004, the share price remained relatively stable (in comparison to the construction period). Even the news of the fire in a freight shuttle on 18 November 1996 caused the share price to fall by only about 10 per cent over the next few days.[16]

By early 2004 it was becoming apparent that the Eurotunnel board were faced with growing criticism from investors. In February 2004 the company announced that it had been forced to make an impairment charge to its fixed assets of £1.3bn. This exceptional charge was designed to bring its reported asset valuation into line with future discounted cash flows. Although Eurotunnel announced Project Galaxie, a radical initiative designed to address the debt problems of the organization, the board were dismissed by a shareholder vote in April 2004.

HOW USEFUL WERE MANAGERS' INCENTIVES AND STATEMENTS TO SHAREHOLDERS?

In any principal–agent relationship, a major concern is the incentives which are provided to the agent to act in a way consistent with the objectives of the principal. In quoted companies, director shareholdings and share options are the traditional mechanisms for motivating the agent. Movements in directors' shareholdings are sometimes taken as an indication of the future prospects of a company. Table 10.2 shows the number of shares held in Eurotunnel by the ten directors who held office continuously between 31 December 1987 and 31 December 1990. Over this three-year period, very little movement occurred in their shareholdings, especially during 1988 and 1989. Only two shareholdings represented more than £10,000 in value at 31 December 1987 and these were held by Malpas (6,010 shares) and Morton (11,500 shares). All directors participated in the November 1990 rights issue except for McMahon and Pennock.

Table 10.2 Eurotunnel directors' shareholdings*

	31.12.87	31.12.88	31.12.89	31.12.90
APJ Bénard	3,010	3,010	3,010	4,816
DM Child	510	510	500	800
Sir Alistair Frame	10	10	10	16
R Lion	–	–	–	3,600
R Malpas	6,010	6,010	6,010	9,616
Sir Kit McMahon	300	300	600	600
Sir Alastair Morton	11,500	11,500	11,500	18,400
Lord Pennock	1,510	1,510	1,500	1,500
Sir Robert Scholey	1,500	1,500	1,500	2,400
B Thiolon	510	510	510	816

*Covering the three-year period 31.12.87 to 31.12.90, during which 10 directors were in office.

Source: Eurotunnel financial statements 1988 to 1991

It would have appeared inconsistent if the directors did not support their company's call for additional equity in November 1990. At the same time, there was clearly no great enthusiasm to take a larger stake in the future of Eurotunnel than was 'required' by the rights issue. The most appropriate conclusion that can be drawn seems to be that the directors were effectively locked into their shareholdings and unable to sell because of the negative signal that such an action would have conveyed to the stock market. The lack of enthusiasm for further purchases (apart from the November 1990 rights issue) could be interpreted as consistent with a general view by the senior management that the prospects for the foreseeable future were not bright. The Annual Report for 1990 (published in April 1991) admitted that 'Eurotunnel started 1990 bordering on insolvency' (p. 6). It is difficult to reconcile such a statement with the extremely high share price in May and June 1989.

The annual accounts also show that from late 1987 executive directors (as well as employees) were entitled to share options. The share options were normally exercisable between 3 and 10 years after being granted. The first options to be exercised by a director are reported in the 1991 annual accounts. During 1991 Bertrand (managing director operations) exercised 40,000 options at an exercise price of 29.96 francs (approximately £3) and sold all the units. This transaction probably realised a substantial gain. Most of the options issued to directors up to 1994 had exercise prices between £2.27 and £3.07. By June 1995 the share price had dipped below £2.00 and, since then, has not risen above that level, which effectively means that the options granted during the period of construction are now valueless.

Was the directors' share option scheme an incentive? Although André Bénard and Sir Alastair Morton (co-chairmen) between them held over 800,000 share options by the end of 1994, they were not exercised and would have lapsed when they resigned from the Eurotunnel board. It is possible that their 'political visibility' meant that they would find it difficult to realize substantial gains on their options before construction was complete. It appears therefore that the share option scheme failed to provide incentives to the top management in such a way that their interests as agents would be aligned sufficiently closely with the interests of the principals. But it is questionable if options should have been designed so they could be exercised before construction had been completed, before all the capital costs had crystallized and before the revenues were known.

The stakeholder group which has fared worst over the history of Eurotunnel is arguably the shareholder group. Not all shareholders, of course, proved to be worse off. Any shareholders who bought at the time of the original *Offer for Sale* or in early 1988 and then sold in the first half of 1989 would have realized substantial capital gains. But the vast majority of shareholders have undoubtedly incurred substantial losses on their investments.

The financial statements provide a historical record, but it seems clear that the share price reacted to events announced in the media, rather than to the financial statements. If the November 1987 *Offer for Sale* document had reported the estimated project cost for each of the years of construction, shareholders might have been in a better position to compare estimated and actual construction costs and appreciate earlier the significant problems faced by Eurotunnel. It is not clear why construction problems and delays known to management in 1988 were not well understood by the market until the second half of 1989. These could have been made known to a wider audience in April 1989, when the 1988 Annual Accounts were published. That could have dampened the excessive share price speculation in May and June 1989. In this respect, the 1988 accounts missed an opportunity to warn existing and potential shareholders of some of the problems facing the project. Several months passed between the agent first becoming aware of construction problems and this information being communicated to the principals. In other words, the interests of the principals would have been better served by more timely information.

EUROTUNNEL PRINCIPAL–AGENT RELATIONSHIP

The agent(s) can be thought of as the board of directors of Eurotunnel, although the concept of agent is dynamic, not static. The most important agents during the period of construction were Bénard and Morton, although they resigned as co-chairmen shortly after completion of construction. Bénard resigned as co-chairman in June 1994 and Morton in October 1996. Both were subsequently appointed honorary life presidents.

By the end of 2003, only one director, Phillippe Lagayette, had been a member of the board at the time of construction, having joined in 1993. In other words, the board of directors dismissed by a shareholder vote in April 2004 could not be held responsible for the construction problems or inaccurate capital and revenue forecasts. However, it appears from press reports in March and April 2004 that it was events pre-1994 that caused such frustration on the part of small shareholders (arising from substantial losses in the value of their shares).

Indeed, it is arguable that the post-1994 management had performed reasonably well under the circumstances, having taken advantage of falling interest rates to reduce the debt burden, and proposing a new initiative, Project Galaxie, which sought to involve the UK and French governments and industry partners in solving the structural problems of Eurotunnel. Indeed, although the rebel shareholders were critical of Project Galaxie, by the end of April 2004 the new Eurotunnel board intended to use the old board's restructuring plan as the basis for its own strategy.[17]

In the same way that the board of directors (as agent) represented a shifting group of actors, the principal(s) represented an even more unstable grouping. Adacte, the shareholder action group, attempted to hold the UK and French governments accountable for the over-optimistic forecasts in the original *Offer for Sale* document. Irrespective of the merits of their arguments, it is likely that, over time, many of the original subscribers would have disposed of their shareholdings. In the unlikely event that the UK and French governments would seriously contemplate compensation, one practical problem would be to identify the original subscribers who had suffered losses and subsequently disposed of their shares.

By the mid-1990s, ample evidence existed to make it clear that Eurotunnel was a risky project, and potential investors could not realistically claim to be unaware of this fact. For example, the Chairmen's letter (dated 7 April 1995) in the Eurotunnel 1994 Annual Report stated 'Eurotunnel is at risk. In 1995 we may succeed or we may fail'.[18] It is consequently interesting to note that on 20 April 2004, after being deposed as chairman of the board, Charles Mackay claimed that over 60 per cent of the shareholders voting against the board had first appeared on the register in 2004.

In addition, it was reported that a Parisian investigating judge was examining whether Nicolas Miguet (a leader of the rebel shareholders) manipulated the share price in 2003 by encouraging investors to buy the stock. It was also reported that 400,000 new shareholders invested in Eurotunnel in the 12 months to March 2004 and that the share price more than doubled between May and September 2003.[19] In summary, not only would it be difficult to make a case for compensation to shareholders by the UK and French governments, it would be difficult from a practical point of view to distinguish between those who had benefited and those who had lost out by investing in Eurotunnel.

DISCUSSION

There is little doubt that in engineering terms Eurotunnel has been an extremely successful project. Thus the 1999 Annual Report refers to the Channel Tunnel being awarded first prize amongst the top 10 construction projects of the 20th century by an international construction panel in the United States.[20] However, 'success' needs to be carefully interpreted in terms of success to the agent or success to the principals. Management (as agent) was arguably successful in achieving completion of the project and therefore maintaining their employment. However, the scale of the cost over-runs was such that ultimately the co-chairmen, Bénard and Morton, resigned shortly after construction was finished. On the other hand, the shareholders (as principals) were noticeably unsuccessful in terms of preventing the substantial declines in net present value of their investments.

The Eurotunnel project raises a number of important issues in terms of principal–agent relationships. Firstly, projected capital costs (on an annual basis) over the construction period 1988 to 1993 were omitted from the original November 1987 *Offer for Sale* document, a prime example of an incomplete contract between principals and agent. The history of large capital projects suggests that, almost invariably, agents tend to underestimate capital costs and overestimate revenues. Including more detailed estimates of the phasing of capital expenditure at the outset would have given the principals an opportunity to monitor actual expenditures compared to predicted expenditures and this would have improved accountability.

Secondly, Eurotunnel has been evolving from a high-risk to a low-risk project. Somewhat paradoxically, its financing structure at the outset (about 80 per cent geared) was more appropriate for a low-risk project. And its eventual financing structure in the future (probably low-geared) will be less suitable for its future status as a utility. Equity (given that dividends can be withheld when necessary) is arguably more appropriate when there is considerable uncertainty attached to a project. However, if a larger proportion of equity had been sought at the outset, then perhaps the project would never have started. It should be remembered that the project received no direct government funding, yet a case for some government backing could be argued on the basis of the wider benefits to the economy of an improved transport infrastructure. It is possible that the promoters (agents) of Eurotunnel were forced to accept a level of financial gearing higher than they would have preferred and, in order to advance the project, tended to err on the side of optimism rather than caution in their predictions.

Thirdly, management incentives were determined at the beginning of the project and turned out to be inappropriate, given the high construction costs. Therefore the share options did not provide sufficient incentives to protect the interests of the shareholders. In addition, the published financial statements, especially during the critical construction period, appeared to provide little new information to the principals as users of accounting information. Instead, major share price movements appeared to stem from events notified to the market outside the traditional financial reporting framework.

Fourthly, as the project matured, there was an increased understanding of all the risks involved. Share price volatility therefore ought to have reduced and this does appear to have happened (with the exception of fluctuations from May to September 2003, referred to above). Nevertheless, it may be the case that, given the past record of over-optimistic forecasts, future expectations of profitability may be substantially discounted by the principals and potential investors. The market may need to see reliable forecasts over a period of time before it fully accepts management (agent) estimates of future profitability, cash flow generation and, ultimately, the payment of dividends.

What are the major uncertainties for the remainder of the concession? They mainly relate to growth of traffic. Until the project opened in 1994, a major uncertainty involved *initial* traffic volumes *plus* growth rates. After operations had started, the area of uncertainty reduced to growth rates (which are also dependent on the actions of competitors). There has also been uncertainty over the amount of debt the banks will want to convert to equity. If the banks convert a relatively large amount, interest charges will be lower but profit available for dividend will be distributed over a larger number of shares (dividend per share will be reduced).

The realization that Eurotunnel is unable to service its debt has focused the attention of all parties on finding a mutually acceptable solution. Although the shareholders have asserted their legal rights by dismissing the board of directors in April 2004, it remains true that, of all the stakeholders, the shareholders potentially have the most to lose. The year 2006, by which time Eurotunnel needs to have in place an agreement with its lenders to refinance its debt, will be the next critical event in the Eurotunnel saga.

Table 10.3 Eurotunnel: key events

14 March 1986	French and UK governments sign concession agreement with Channel Tunnel Group Ltd and France Manche SA to last for 55 years
29 July 1987	Fixed link treaty ratified between France and UK in 'Treaty of Canterbury'
16 November 1987	Offer for Sale of 220m units @ £3.50 raises £770m
1 December 1987	Excavating starts
June 1989	Share price peaks at £11.64
July 1989	Eurotunnel announces that forecast cost to completion is likely to exceed the funds committed to the Project
30 October 1990	UK–French contact by a probe in the service tunnel –first land contact in recorded history between Britain and Continental Europe
2 November 1990	Rights issue raises £570m
11 October 1993	Eurotunnel says £1bn more needed
10 December 1993	Contractors hand over tunnel
6 May 1994	Official opening ceremony
May 1994	Rights issue of 324m units @ £2.65 per unit raises £816m
14 September 1995	'Standstill' – Eurotunnel suspends payment of interest on its main debt in order to renegotiate the group's financing
30 January 1998	Eurotunnel announces that the 174-strong banking syndicate had signed an agreement to carry out an £8.5bn restructuring
9 February 2004	Eurotunnel announces Project Galaxie, containing proposals to resolve high debt levels and under-utilization of infrastructure
7 April 2004	Charles Mackay (chairman) and Richard Shirrefs (chief executive) sacked by shareholder vote at AGM

Discussion questions

1 Do Eurotunnel's shareholders deserve to be compensated for their losses?
2 Discuss the proposition that agents have an incentive to be optimistic when proposing large capital projects.
3 Which stakeholders were most adversely affected by Eurotunnel's financial difficulties?
4 Briefly outline the causes of Eurotunnel's financial problems. Could, or should, these problems have been foreseen?
5 'Eurotunnel has been both a success and a disaster'. Discuss.

REFERENCES

Eurotunnel (1987) *Offer for Sale*, November. London: Eurotunnel.
Eurotunnel (1990) *Rights Issue*, November. London: Eurotunnel.
Eurotunnel (1994) *Rights Issue*, May. London: Eurotunnel.
Eurotunnel (1997) *Financial Restructuring Proposals*, May. London: Eurotunnel.
Holliday, I., Marcou, G. and Vickerman, R. (1991) *The Channel Tunnel: Public Policy, Regional Development and European Integration*. London: Belhaven Press.
Shleifer, A. and Vishny, R.W. (1997) 'A survey of corporate governance', *Journal of Finance*, Vol. 52, No. 2 (June): 737–83.

NOTES

1 This chapter is co-authored with Carmen A. Li, Economics Department, University of Essex.

2 See Holliday, Marcou and Vickerman, 1991: 1.

3 *Sunday Times*, 16 April 1995, Business Focus: 3.

4 Given that rights issues were made in 1990 and 1994, the capital loss to investors was somewhat smaller than that implied by this comparison, but nevertheless substantial. An investor in the original 1987 *Offer for Sale* suffered a capital loss of almost 90 per cent by the end of April 2004. The only compensation consisted of travel privileges once the project began operations in 1994.

5 *Financial Times*, 9 August 1997

6 *Financial Times*, 9 August 1997.

7 *Financial Times*, 6 May 1994.

8 See interview with Graham Corbett, Eurotunnel Finance Director, as reported in *Accountancy Age*, January 1991: 40.

9 *Accountancy Age*, January 1991: 41.

10 *Financial Times*, 6 May 1994.

11 In December 1993 the French and UK governments agreed to extend the original expiry date of the concession from 2042 to 2052.

12 *Sunday Times*, 16 April 1995.

13 *Financial Times*, 29 November 1997.

14 Strictly speaking, transactions in the equity of Eurotunnel are based on 'units' of equity where a unit equals one share in Eurotunnel PLC twinned with one share in Eurotunnel SA. However, for the purposes of this paper, reference to the share price of Eurotunnel should be understood to mean the units traded on the London Stock Exchange.

15 Quoted in the *Sunday Times*, 16 April 1995.

16 It is quite probable that the share price from 1996 onwards was being maintained by the individual shareholders who held travel privileges dating back to the original *Offer for Sale* in 1987. Travel privileges were also available to new investors holding a minimum of 1,000 shares.

17 *Financial Times*, 23 April 2004.

18 Eurotunnel, *Annual Report 1994*: 5.

19 *Financial Times*, 21 April 2004.

20 Eurotunnel, *Annual Report 1999*: 1.

Barings

February 1995 proved to be a turning point in public attitudes to financial risk in the UK with the collapse of Barings Bank. The bank had been in business for over 200 years and still retained strong connections with the founding family. Barings had been founded in the eighteenth century by Francis Baring, son of a German immigrant. Before long, Barings was highly thought of in financial circles, as shown by the fact that in 1803 Barings were involved in negotiations on behalf of the USA to purchase Louisiana from France.

Barings grew steadily until the end of the nineteenth century and extended its operations to South America. Under the chairmanship of Lord Revelstoke, in 1890 the bank was very nearly bankrupted, because of Revelstoke's speculative ventures in Argentina. But the Bank of England and Barings' competitors such as the Rothschilds were well aware that such a collapse could have repercussions for the entire banking system and Barings was not allowed to go under. Barings was refinanced and reorganized from a partnership into a limited company. The events of 1890 were a salutary lesson to the bank, which subsequently worked hard to re-establish a reputation for reliability and security in the banking world.

As the capital markets became bigger and more complex during the 1970s and 1980s, Barings responded by setting up Baring Securities to take advantage of new and profitable opportunities in the increasingly sophisticated financial markets. However, the separation of the traditional merchant banking from the new, more glamorous, brokerage activities seems to have led to tensions and conflicts in the Barings group. And it is quite possible that the difficulties the group encountered in the 1990s may have been partly due to this 'clash of cultures' and the fact that many people at Barings simply did not understand the potentially huge losses that could result from poorly controlled derivatives trading. But Baring Securities was to be the group's downfall. Despite the collapse in 1995, the name of Barings carries on, following the bank's takeover by the Dutch bank ING (International Nederlanden Group). ING Barings survives, but the connection with the Baring family has been largely lost.

NICK LEESON

From the public's point of view, the collapse of Barings' Bank is closely connected with the name of Nick Leeson, the derivatives trader who worked for the Singapore branch of Baring Securities. Leeson had joined Barings in July 1989 in the settlement department, and quickly proved efficient at completing the paperwork once a brokerage transaction had been made. Efficient settlement work is essential to a broking company since – even though it is a technical function, carried out after the broking transaction has been completed – it is vital to ensure the correct amounts ultimately pass between the buyer and seller of the securities and to any financial intermediaries. Leeson appeared to get on well in Barings, and in 1990 he was given the opportunity to take care of a problem that had arisen in the Jakarta, Indonesia office of Baring Securities.

During most of 1990, Leeson – with his future wife Lisa, who had also been employed by Baring Securities – sorted through a substantial amount of documentation, including share certificates and bearer bonds, which had been badly neglected by the Jakarta settlement office. As a result, Leeson gained a reputation for having a thorough understanding of the brokerage settlement process. According to Leeson himself:

> I returned to London in March 1991, and from then on was seen as the settlements expert in futures and options. I had patience and stamina, I applied painstaking logic, and I knew that in the end I could sort out any problem. I got my head down and stuck to it, and I wasn't afraid of asking the most stupid questions. People at the London end of Barings were all so know-all that nobody dared ask a stupid question in case they looked silly in front of everyone else. I always found that the most basic, obvious questions are the ones which are most difficult to answer, and which normally bring out the crucial piece of missing knowledge. (Leeson with Whitley, 1997: 38).

In less than three years Leeson had established a positive reputation with the Barings management.

At the beginning of 1992, Baring Securities decided to set up a futures operation in Singapore to take advantage of the growing success of SIMEX (Singapore International Monetary Exchange). Nick Leeson seemed to be the right person to head up the operation and, in April 1992, Nick and Lisa Leeson moved to Singapore. Leeson was appointed general manager of Baring Futures (Singapore) and was responsible for organizing the settlements and accounting departments and acting as head of the SIMEX trading operations.

The true extent of Barings' problems was not to be fully appreciated until February 1995. But even in 1992 there was a warning signal of potential problems ahead. Before he took up the posting to Singapore, Leeson had applied to the SFA (Securities and Futures Authority) for a City of

London trading licence. Despite his success with the settlements part of broking activities (often referred to as the 'back office'), Leeson was keen to be involved in the more glamorous side of broking, that is dealing in futures and options (referred to as the 'front office'). In broking circles, those who worked in the back office were almost regarded as second-class citizens compared to the front office. In the front office there was greater opportunity to earn sizeable bonuses, which came to be a feature of city financial institutions during the 1980s. Leeson would not be able to actively trade securities unless he was licensed by the SFA.

Baring Securities therefore submitted Leeson's application to the SFA. According to Rawnsley (1996), Leeson had answered 'no' to a question whether he had any County Court judgments outstanding against him. Following a routine check by the SFA, it was found that Leeson indeed did have an outstanding judgment. In fact, in May 1992 Watford County Court, on behalf of National Westminster Bank, made a judgment of £2,426 against him. The SFA returned the application to Baring Securities, who simply withdrew the application. It seems that no more was said about the misinformation and there was no negative impact on Leeson's career, since he moved to Singapore shortly afterwards. Leeson was to remain in Singapore, working for Baring Securities, for almost three years.

When Leeson arrived in Singapore in 1992, he was just 25 years old. During 1992 it seems that Baring Futures (Singapore) was operating profitably, buying and selling futures and options on behalf of clients, and also for Fernando Gueler who was head of futures and options trading in Tokyo. Leeson spent his mornings from Monday to Friday overseeing dealing at SIMEX and afternoons were spent reconciling the trades, working through the dealing slips. On busy days the settlement process could take until midnight.

ERROR ACCOUNT 88888

However, given the sometimes frenetic activity on the dealing floor at SIMEX, it was not unknown for errors to take place. These were often no more than misunderstandings. Normally the bank would accept the loss, on the assumption that the client had acted in good faith. An error account, 99905, had been created in which the relevant transactions could be put until they had been resolved or else written off in the profit-and-loss account. According to Leeson, he was asked by the London office of Barings to create another error account, to handle only trivial items arising in Singapore. Consequently, error account 88888 was created, this unusual number being chosen because in Chinese the number 8 is supposed to be lucky.

But within a few weeks, the London office of Barings decided that it needed to see all errors arising in Singapore and that its computers could cope with the numbers of errors being recorded. Leeson was therefore asked to revert back to using only error account 99905. The new error account 88888 therefore lay dormant. But according to Leeson, he first used it seriously on Friday 17 July 1992. One of his employees had misunderstood a client's orders and instead of buying 20 contracts had instead *sold* 20 contracts. To rectify the mistake, Barings would need to *buy* 20 contracts to cancel out the original mistake and on top of that *buy a further* 20 contracts to satisfy the client's order. The hit to Barings' profit-and-loss account amounted to about £20,000.

Because Leeson discovered the mistake on Friday 17 July after close of trading at SIMEX he was not able to rectify the situation until trading restarted on the following Monday, by which time the market price could have moved against him. In order to hide the mistake Leeson made use of account 88888. Leeson was reportedly annoyed that his superior in Singapore – Simon Jones, Operations Manager for South Asia – had not allowed him to employ sufficient qualified staff to cope with the expanding volume of work. When Leeson asked Simon Jones for advice on resolving the 20 contracts, he advised him to sack the employee and inform Andrew Bayliss, Deputy Chairman of Baring Securities in London.

Leeson did not take Simon Jones' advice and instead used the account 88888 to mask the error. His justification was that he needed time to think how to hide the loss and also he wanted to protect his staff. It is also possible that he was not keen for Barings in London to learn of this type of mistake, which could damage his reputation. The problem was that Leeson found it remarkably easy to hide errors in this way, and this was facilitated by the fact that he was in charge of both the 'front office' and 'back office' for Barings Singapore operation:

> Over the next few months, up to the end of 1992, I put over thirty errors into the 88888 account. This was bad, but not catastrophic. There were other errors in the London account, but I put into 88888 the particularly large discrepancies which I thought would get my newly recruited traders into trouble. There was no hard and fast rule – an error's an error – but the traders knew that if they'd made a bad mistake they could refer it to me, and then it would find its way into the 88888 account. (Leeson with Whitley, 1997: 63)

LEESON'S TRADING AT SIMEX

In 1992 Leeson applied for a SIMEX trading licence, which would allow him onto the trading floor at SIMEX to act as a trader. He passed the SIMEX exams late in 1992 and was granted a trading licence. From Barings' viewpoint, having Leeson as a trader was useful because he could take clients on a tour of the SIMEX trading floor. This created a dangerous conflict of interest, since Leeson could now act as a trader and at the same time be responsible for the accounting of those trades in the 'back office'. Although he was supposed to trade only on behalf of clients, executing their orders, he soon began to start trading on his own behalf, and he was able to cover up these activities using the 88888 account.

During the first half of 1993 Leeson's losses, due to his unauthorized but hidden trading activities, began to climb. At one stage they reached £6m according to his account. At first, he seems to have been unnerved at the sheer size of the accumulating losses. One of his attempts to reduce these losses involved selling 'straddles'. A straddle combines a put (buy) option with a call (sell) option at an identical strike price. The benefit to Leeson was that he would receive premium income when the options were written. The downside was that if the market moved significantly away from the strike price (either up or down) then the other party would exercise their right to buy or sell. This strategy would only be profitable for Leeson if the market price stayed close to the strike price over time, but was also particularly risky because Leeson did not cover himself by hedging the position. But Leeson claims that he was lucky and by July 1993 had managed to clear his losses and bring the 88888 account back to zero.

But it was not long before Leeson was tempted to repeat his unauthorized trading. He had established a reputation as a star trader. He was earning £50,000 a year plus a bonus based on his 1992 trading of over £100,000. He was reluctant to lose the reputation he had acquired and he returned to his old tactics of hiding his trading losses in account 88888.

Barings had previously passed over an opportunity to make such illegal trading impossible. At the time the Singapore operation had been set up, James Bax, who was Regional Manager of Barings South Asia, had sent a memo to Andrew Fraser, Managing Director of Baring Securities in London:

> My concern is that once again we are in danger of setting up a structure which will subsequently prove disastrous and with which we will succeed in losing either a lot of money or client goodwill or probably both . . . In my view it is critical that we should keep clear reporting lines, and if this office is involved in SIMEX at all, then Nick Leeson should report to Simon Jones and then be responsible for the operations side. (Leeson with Whitley, 1997: 88–9)

It is clear that James Bax was concerned about the conflict of interest involved if there was not a clear demarcation between the 'front office' and the 'back office'. Leeson subsequently acknowledged that if the advice of Bax had been followed, such that Leeson had responsibility only for the settlements and accounting, he would not have been able to instruct the traders in the way he did, let alone indulge in trading himself.

Why did Barings ignore the advice of James Bax? It is possible that Barings was keen to restrict costs. If we are to believe Leeson's version of events, he was having problems getting authority from Barings to recruit sufficient numbers of well qualified staff. It was also possible, that over time, as the Singapore operation appeared to be making excellent profits, that Leeson's superiors were reluctant to annoy Leeson by requesting him to curtail his trading activities which might have led to their 'star trader' resigning and moving to another broking firm. According to Leeson:

> As my losses in Error Account 88888 began to creep up again from the zero balance I had managed to achieve in July, I found myself growing increasingly angry that I hadn't shut the whole thing down and never used it again. I began to trade aggressively to make the money back, and these trades never turned out the right way for me. (Leeson with Whitley, 1997, p. 89)

Leeson's losses continued to increase during 1993 and into 1994, but he had become adept at hiding them in error account 88888. Consequently it appeared to Barings that Leeson was a particularly successful trader, because they were aware of his profitable trades but not his loss-making activities. However, under the SIMEX regulations he was having to request Barings London to provide him with increasingly large amounts of cash to cover his margin calls. The margin calls were required under the SIMEX system as a deposit or form of collateral in respect of Barings' trades.

It seems that for some time Leeson was able to hide his deception by exploiting differences among his seniors in London. Ron Baker was head of derivatives trading at Baring Brothers and Mary Walz was head of equity derivatives trading. Their focus was on the profit-and-loss account and growing the brokerage business and, according to Leeson, they were keen to ensure that their bonuses at the year-end would be maximized. But Tony Hawes, Treasurer of Baring Investment Bank, and Tony Railton, Futures and Options Settlement Clerk at Baring Securities, were concerned at the increasingly large requirements Leeson was making to London in respect of margin calls. Once again, staff at Barings were ignoring warning signals which could have been detected from the extreme demands for cash emanating from the Singapore operation. Despite Leeson's attempts to disguise the extent of his funding request, 'the funding continued to escalate; the cumulative funding of Baring Futures (Singapore) which stood at £221 million on 31 December 1994 had reached an epic £742 million by 24 February. This represented more than twice the reported capital of the Barings Group' (Rawnsley, 1996: 176–7).

LEESON RESORTS TO FORGERY

As Leeson's unauthorized trading losses increased, he became increasingly desperate to disguise the deception. In January 1995, Leeson attempted to claim that sums would be receivable from SIMEX but that a delay had occurred because an OTC (over-the-counter) trade had been incorrectly booked. Over-the-counter trades are trades conducted outside a recognized stock exchange. Leeson claimed that an amount of £50m (outstanding since December 1994) was due from Spear, Leeds and Kellogg, a reputable broking firm which specialized in derivatives. Barings' auditors in London, Coopers and Lybrand, needed an explanation for what had happened and also needed to see documentation that would support Leeson's claim.

Leeson looked through his old correspondence and came across a letter from Richard Hogan who was Managing Director at Spear, Leeds and Kellogg. Leeson then arranged for two notes to be typed out on plain paper. The first was allegedly from Ron Baker, Head of Derivatives Trading at Baring Brothers in London. This fraudulent note purportedly confirmed that he knew and approved of the deal with Spear, Leeds and Kellogg. Leeson then composed a second fraudulent note, allegedly from Spear, Leeds and Kellogg, which confirmed that payment would be made to Barings on 2 February 1995. Leeson then proceeded to cut out the signatures of Ron Baker and Richard Hogan and paste them on to the forged notes and photocopied them onto the appropriate headed paper.

The next step was to have these forged letters faxed to Barings' Singapore office. Leeson arranged this by taking the forged letters home and sent the two letters from his home fax machine to Barings' Singapore fax machine. Interestingly, Leeson did not remember how his home fax machine had been set up and he had forgotten that when the forged documents arrived at the Barings Singapore office, they were headed up with a line 'From Nick & Lisa'.[1] This was a serious miscalculation on Leeson's part, but the oversight was apparently not picked up. Leeson also arranged for a transfer of £50m from one Citibank account to another and requested a statement from Citibank to show the £50m balance, before the meaningless transaction was reversed. Leeson now had additional 'documentation' which purportedly showed that the £50m had actually been received by Barings Singapore.

Until this point, Leeson might have been able to bluff his way out of trouble and even claim that he had innocently got out of his depth with the derivatives trading, but – as he later recounted –

> once I'd forged these two documents, I knew that I was damned. These were forgeries. Up until now I had prevaricated, been economical with the truth, refused to separate out numbers which others could have easily found, and made outrageous claims for funding from London. If I had to stand in front of a jury, I'd have confessed to false accounting and probably obtaining property by deception. But now I'd added a new crime to this catalogue. I couldn't say that anyone else was responsible. I couldn't pass it off as a white lie, needed at the time. I had physically cut out somebody's signature, glued it to a piece of paper, taken it to my flat, faxed it back to myself, and now I was going to hand it to Rachel Yong to pass on to the auditors. (Leeson with Whitley, 1997: 238–9)

RUMOURS IN THE MARKET

By early 1995, the huge trading volumes generated by Leeson's dealing activities on SIMEX were leading to rumours and doubts about Barings' financial position. Observers of the market started speculating about the identity of Barings' clients. It seems to have been assumed that Barings was not trading on its own account (proprietary trading), but must have been acting on behalf of a wealthy client. Rawnsley (1996: 174) quotes sources who believed that Barings were trading on behalf of American hedge funds or possibly a Japanese client who was in financial difficulties. It has also been suggested that Leeson intimated that he was receiving backing from George Soros, the international financier who had made his reputation in 1992 when he speculated against sterling and correctly anticipated that sterling would be forced out of the European exchange-rate mechanism.

In January 1995, The Bank for International Settlements in Basle had been concerned about market rumours that Barings would not be able to meet its margin funding commitments. According to Rawnsley (1996: 175), the managing director of Salomon Brothers Hong Kong – who had previously been head of Baring Securities Hong Kong – contacted Barings in February 1995 because he was concerned that Barings, or a client of Barings, were about to be bankrupted. However, Barings assured him that there was no exposure.

During January 1995, Leeson had increasingly resorted to straddles in order to receive premium income. According to Gapper and Denton (1996: 281), there were 65,000 options in the 88888 account that were based on the Nikkei index. The Nikkei (or Nikkei 225) is an index of the leading 225 stocks traded on the Tokyo Stock Exchange. In terms of risk, this was reckoned to be equivalent to owning £1.8 billion in shares. The strike price of these contracts averaged 19,200, which meant that Leeson would benefit most when the Nikkei index stood at 19,200. Any deviation from 19,200, either up or down, increased Leeson's losses.

THE KOBE EARTHQUAKE

Leeson's hopes of pursuing a profitable strategy and somehow trading himself out of trouble were badly shaken by a devastating earthquake in Kobe, Japan, on 17 January 1995. This proved to be one of the most severe earthquakes in Japan for a number of years and caused considerable loss of life and damage to property. The Nikkei index fell at first but not as far as some had predicted. It seems that the market was uncertain about the eventual impact of the earthquake on the Nikkei index. For instance, if the Japanese government decided to implement a substantial reconstruction programme, this could have a long-term positive impact on the Japanese economy, and therefore on the Nikkei index. Falls in the Nikkei index were alarming for Leeson, who then attempted to buy futures on the Nikkei index. He increasingly bought contracts in the hope that he could keep the Nikkei index close to his target of 19,200.

At first his strategy appeared to work. But speculators soon became pessimistic about the prospects for the Japanese economy and in one day alone the Nikkei fell by 1,175 points. Amazingly, Leeson was still able to report some profits to Barings, and maintain his image of a successful trader. However, the reality was that he had lost approximately £100m in the space of about 10 days following the Kobe earthquake. Fernando Gueler, Head of Futures and Options Trading for Baring Securities in Japan, simply could not understand how Leeson was apparently able to trade at a profit during this period. Gueler did not suspect that Leeson's positions were not hedged and was only to learn the truth later in February 1995.

THE FINAL WEEKS

As February 1995 progressed, matters became increasingly desperate. Tony Railton, Futures and Options Settlement Clerk with Baring Securities, based in London, had arrived in Singapore and was asking Leeson for documentation on the supposed OTC trade that had occurred in December 1994 and led to the shortfall of £50m. Leeson tried to fend off Railton's request, saying that the auditors, Coopers and Lybrand, were in possession of the relevant papers, implying that Railton would need to request the documentation from the auditors. Leeson had been requested by Baring Securities in London to reduce his trading positions, but he continued, nevertheless, to request large amounts of funding from London for his SIMEX margin commitments.

Leeson attempted to keep up the pretence of successful trading through February, knowing that at the end of February 1995 Barings would determine the bonuses to be paid to staff based on the previous financial year's results. It was rumoured that Peter Baring, chairman of Barings, would receive a bonus of £1m. Barings had a particularly generous bonus system in which half of the pre-tax profits were paid out as an incentive to staff. This percentage was much higher than most other banks in the UK. It seemed as if Leeson himself would be due for a bonus of £450,000 on top of his annual salary. It seems that Leeson's strategy, therefore, would have been to attempt to stay with Barings, collect his bonus and then resign. However, Leeson must have realized that, following his resignation, Barings would pursue him for the return of the bonus.

Leeson's last day of work for Barings was Thursday 23 February 1995. The Nikkei index had slumped and Leeson was patently disobeying instructions from London to reduce his trading positions. After the morning's trading, during which Leeson had continued to buy futures to support the Nikkei index, Leeson returned to his office. Tony Railton again asked for a meeting, together with Simon Jones, to discuss the missing money. During the course of the meeting, Leeson made an excuse and said he would return later. Instead he simply went home, leaving Barings Singapore for the last time. The following day, Friday 24 February, Nick Leeson and Lisa were in Kuala Lumpur, Malaysia, from where Leeson sent a brief handwritten fax to James Bax and Simon Jones in Singapore. In the fax, Leeson apologized for the predicament that he had left them in and said that he was resigning with immediate effect from Barings.

On the evening of Thursday 23 February, Railton and Jones had attempted to reconcile Leeson's accounts. Railton phoned Barings London to express his concerns and Peter Norris called a meeting with some executives to discuss Leeson's disappearance. When the 88888 account was discovered, a quick calculation suggested that Barings could be facing losses of at least £200m. Already it seemed that Barings were on the verge of collapse since the group's combined equity and loan capital amounted to just over £400m.

RESCUE ATTEMPTS

On the morning of Friday 24 February, Peter Baring contacted the Bank of England. Although one of the Bank of England's tasks was to try to anticipate if any financial institutions were in trouble, the news from Peter Baring that Barings were facing financial collapse seemed to come as a complete shock to the Bank of England. The Bank of England then contacted a number of bankers who might be able to fund a rescue and called a meeting for the evening of Friday 24 February. The banks were well aware that their own reputations could be damaged if Barings was allowed to go under. By Saturday 25 February (coincidentally Leeson's birthday), Barings' estimated losses had climbed to £385m. A meeting with the Chancellor of the Exchequer confirmed that the government was not willing to give financial support to a rescue.

Barings desperately tried to organize a rescue bid over the weekend of Saturday and Sunday 25/26 February. By Sunday 26 February, news about Barings' problems was beginning to appear in the newspapers. Barings' last hope for survival came from representatives of the Brunei Investment Agency who indicated they might contribute towards the rescue. By this time it was thought that £600m would be needed to recapitalize the bank. However, the Brunei Investment Agency concluded that the risks were too large and that there was insufficient time to properly consider a proposed rescue.

Barings' total losses eventually amounted to £830m. Barings was taken over by ING and restructured. Peter Baring (chairman) and Andrew Tuckey (deputy chairman) both resigned and ING requested the resignation of a number of managers. Most of the staff of Barings retained their jobs but the bond holders lost most of the value of their investment.

OFFICIAL REPORTS AND THE AFTERMATH

On 19 July 1995 in London, the Board of Banking Supervision issued a report referring to 'a failure of controls of management and other internal controls of the most basic kind'.[2] Much of the blame was attributed to Norris and Baker, and Baker told investigators 'There is no doubt in my mind that my lack of experience in the area was a contributing factor to what happened'.[3] In addition Coopers and Lybrand were criticized for failing to detect Leeson's fraud. The Bank of England report concluded that Barings' collapse was due to the unauthorized activities of one individual, Nick Leeson, but these activities had not been detected by management due to internal control failures of a most basic kind.

A report by the Singapore authorities, published in October 1995, was more critical of Barings' executives, in particular Peter Norris, Head of Investment Banking, and James Bax, Regional Manager for South Asia (Rawnsley, 1996). Norris was described as 'untruthful' in the report. In addition, Norris and Bax were accused of playing down the importance of the £50m discrepancy related to the purported Spear, Leeds and Kellogg transaction and of actively discouraging investigations.

Nick and Lisa Leeson had attempted to escape from Malaysia back to London. Although they managed to leave Malaysia, they could not take a direct flight to London but had to break their journey in Germany and Leeson was arrested at Frankfurt airport on Thursday 2 March. Leeson attempted to fight extradition back to Singapore for several months, fearing that he would receive a lengthy prison sentence from the Singapore authorities. His hope was that he would be returned to London to face trial and possibly a lighter sentence. However, the Serious Fraud Office seemed to be reluctant to press charges against Leeson and eventually in November 1995 he returned to Singapore. In December 1995 Leeson pleaded guilty to two counts of deceiving the Barings' auditors and cheating SIMEX. He was sentenced to six and a half years in jail, the sentence being backdated to March 1995 when he had been arrested in Germany awaiting extradition. He was released early for good behaviour in 1999 and then he returned to the UK.

In Singapore, Baring Futures' books had been audited by the local firm of Deloitte and Touche. In London, Coopers and Lybrand audited the London books of Baring Futures. KPMG, who were appointed as liquidators following the collapse of Barings, started proceedings against Deloitte and Touche (Singapore). In 2003 the High Court in London found that officers of Barings Bank, rather than Deloitte and Touche (Singapore), were responsible for the failure to detect fraudulent trading by Nick Leeson. The High Court decision in 2003 required Deloitte to pay just £1.5m in damages as a result of negligence on relatively technical counts. This was a tiny fraction of the £131m damages originally sought by Barings. The litigation was finally concluded[4] in April 2004 at the Court of Appeal in London, when KPMG and Deloitte reached a settlement.

DISCUSSION

It is interesting to speculate why Leeson allowed his unauthorized trading activities to continue for so long. By his own account he suspected that it was only a matter of time before he was found out, which in some ways would be a relief for him. But he was perhaps surprised by the success of his own deceptions and his explanations to the Barings staff and auditors. The Kobe earthquake in January 1995 and its impact on the Nikkei index cannot be seen as a main cause of Leeson's and Barings' problems, although no doubt it accelerated the collapse of the bank. It does not seem that Leeson intended to enrich himself massively as a result of his dealings. Shortly after the Barings crash, Leeson was referred to by Eddie George, Governor of the Bank of England, as a 'rogue trader' and this phrase captured the public's attention. However, the phrase was possibly an attempt to signal that one person, Nick Leeson, should shoulder the blame for what had happened.

It is somewhat curious that the Bank of England was taken completely by surprise by the final collapse of Barings. Doubts have been expressed as to how effective the Bank of England Report was and Rawnsley (1996: 205) argues that 'The Bank of England . . . let itself off too lightly in its own analysis of the collapse. While the Board of Banking Supervision's report was liberal in its blame, spreading it lavishly around Barings management and its auditors as well as Leeson, the Bank itself came off relatively unscathed'. Gapper and Denton (1996) seem to agree and state that the Bank of England had avoided a rigorous inquiry by having the collapse investigated by the Board of Banking Supervision. Eddie George (Governor of the Bank of England) and Brian Quinn (Executive Director of the Bank of England) were both members of the Board of Banking Supervision. But Eddie George had argued that the inquiry would be fair because he and Quinn would not take part in drawing up conclusions about the Bank of England.

Table 11.1 Barings: key events

1989	Nick Leeson joins Barings
1992	Baring Securities set up futures operation in Singapore; Leeson is appointed general manager of Baring Futures (Singapore); Leeson hides some contracts in error account 88888; Leeson is authorized to act as a trader at SIMEX
1993	Leeson's losses on account 88888 increase, although he clears the account to zero by July; but losses on account increase again during second half of year
1994	Losses on account 88888 continue to climb; Leeson claims £50 million debt is owed from Spear, Leeds and Kellogg (December); Leeson begins to forge supporting documentation
January 1995	Earthquake hits Kobe, Japan and Nikkei 225 falls; Leeson increases his trading activities in an attempt to recoup his losses
February 1995	Leeson leaves Singapore (23 February); UK news media report Barings' financial problems (26 February); Barings ceases trading (27 February)
March 1995	Leeson arrested in Germany
July 1995	Board of Banking Supervision in London reports on Barings collapse
December 1995	Leeson sentenced to six and a half years in jail in Singapore

Discussion questions

1 How would you apportion blame for Barings' collapse among Nick Leeson, the senior management, the auditors and the regulatory authorities?

2 Discuss the basic internal control failures referred to in the Bank of England report.

3 What lessons do you believe can be learned from Barings' collapse?

4 Does the Barings saga make it more likely or less likely that these events could be repeated?

5 Is it reasonable to suggest 'corporate greed' as an explanation for Barings' collapse?

6 Which stakeholders were most badly affected by the collapse of Barings?

REFERENCES

Board of Banking Supervision (1995) *Inquiry into the Circumstances of the Collapse of Barings*. London: HMSO.

Gapper, J. and Denton, N. (1996) *All That Glitters: The Fall of Barings*. London: Hamish Hamilton.

Leeson, N. with Whitley, E. (1997) *Rogue Trader*. London: Warner Books.

Rawnsley, J. (1996) *Going for Broke: Nick Leeson and the Collapse of Barings Bank*. London: HarperCollins.

NOTES

1 Gapper and Denton, 1996: 305.
2 Gapper and Denton, 1996: 336.
3 Gapper and Denton, 1996: 336.
4 *Financial Times*, 23 April 2004: 5.

Shell

TWELVE

Shell or Royal Dutch/Shell has a fascinating history. The company popularly known as 'Shell', more correctly referred to as the Royal Dutch/Shell Group,[1] can trace its origins back to early nineteenth-century London where Marcus Samuel opened a shop to sell seashells to natural-history enthusiasts.[2] The venture developed into an import–export business and in the 1890s Marcus's son began exporting lighting and heating oil to the Far East. The Shell Transport and Trading Company was formed in 1897. At about the same time a Dutch competitor, the Royal Dutch company, was developing oil fields in Asia. A merger of the two organizations in 1907 led to the formation of the Royal Dutch/Shell Group of companies.

Royal Dutch/Shell continued to develop in the twentieth century and has proved to be one of the most enduring and successful global corporations. Whereas other companies which were at one time household names have now been relegated to the lower divisions of the corporate league table, Royal Dutch/Shell has for decades maintained a position among the top handful of leading global corporations. Also of interest is the stability of the group in terms of its company names and operations, which have remained focused on the energy industry, though the group has acted to innovate when necessary, for instance in the development of natural gas as an alternative energy source. The shell brand name and logo seem to symbolize the stability of the group and the pecten symbol is more or less unchanged from the early twentieth century.

The Royal Dutch/Shell Group sees itself mainly as an energy group and employs 119,000 people in 145 countries.[3] Its main activities are exploration and production of gas and power, oil products and chemicals. During the 1990s it received adverse publicity as a result of environmental concerns, first from its operations in Nigeria and then from its North Sea operations. Shell had intended to sink the Brent Spar oil platform in the North Sea, but the intervention of Greenpeace raised public concern about possible pollution from dumping the oil platform, despite the fact that Shell had received UK government approval to do this. Eventually in 1998 Shell arranged to have the oil platform broken up in Norway.[4]

Unlike some other cases in this book, Shell is not, nor is it likely to be, in danger of corporate collapse. The focus of this case concerns Shell's booking of oil and gas reserves, which first came to public attention in early 2004. Undoubtedly this was a serious matter for the company, and for Sir Philip Watts, chairman of the committee of managing directors, and Walter van de Vijver, head of exploration and production, who both resigned on 3 March 2004. Then in April 2004, Judy Boynton, chief financial officer, was asked to resign. But in order to understand how these events came about, it is useful to look at the structure of the group.

GROUP STRUCTURE

The overall group has two parent companies: Royal Dutch Petroleum Company (based in the Netherlands) and Shell Transport and Trading Company plc (based in the United Kingdom). Royal Dutch Petroleum represents a 60 per cent interest in the group and Shell Transport and Trading represents an interest of 40 per cent. The two parent companies are not directly involved in commercial operations themselves but receive income in the form of dividends from other units in the group. The income from the companies in the group is split, with Royal Dutch Petroleum taking 60 per cent and Shell Transport and Trading taking 40 per cent.

Beneath the parent companies – and jointly owned by them – are the two group holding companies, Shell Petroleum NV (based in the Netherlands) and Shell Petroleum Company Limited (based in the United Kingdom). These two group holding companies hold all the group interests in the service and operating companies. One of the most important committees in the group is known as the Committee of Managing Directors. In 2004 this body was headed by Jeroen van der Veer, who succeeded Sir Philip Watts on 3 March 2004 as chairman of the Committee of Managing Directors. The next most important person in the organization in 2004 was Malcolm Brinded, vice-chairman of the Committee of Managing Directors, who succeeded Walter van de Vijver on 3 March 2004 as chief executive of exploration and production.

The board structures are somewhat different for the two parent companies, due to the different influences of Dutch company law and practice as against UK company law and practice.[5] Royal Dutch Petroleum has a two-tier structure in which the supervisory function is intended to emphasize the strategic direction of the group, while the management function is identified more closely with day-to-day operations. The supervisory board – six directors plus the chairman, at that time Aad Jacobs – controls the overall direction of the organization, is responsible for ensuring that appropriate systems are in place and oversees the work of the management board, which, as its name implies, is responsible for managing the business and providing financial and management information to the supervisory board. There is a clear de jure hierarchy, with the supervisory board above the board of management, which at this time consisted of two men: Jeroen van der Veer, President of Royal Dutch, and Rob Routs, Managing Director of Royal Dutch and Group Managing Director.

The board structure for Shell Transport and Trading is quite different and follows the normal practice for UK companies, which is a unitary board. The members or directors of Shell Transport and Trading are either executive directors or non-executive directors. It is not, strictly speaking, wholly accurate to say that the non-executive directors – in Shell's case, Lord Oxburgh, the chairman, and eight others – are the equivalent of the supervisory board on the Dutch side. But in practice, the role of the non-executive directors is to ensure that the overall strategy of the business is appropriate and to take on a large degree of responsibility in relation to matters such as audit, nomination of new directors and remuneration of directors. The executive director – Shell Transport and Trading had only one, Malcolm Brinded, the Managing Director – is responsible for day-to-day operations. Although attempts are made to distinguish between 'strategic' and 'tactical' decisions, in practice these areas are often blurred. For instance, pricing policy could have implications for the overall direction of the group, if it were aggressive and allowed the company to enter new markets, and therefore could be viewed as 'strategic'. On the other hand some pricing policy decisions, perhaps merely responding to cost increases, would not be regarded as 'strategic' but instead 'tactical' and capable of being left to the management board or executive directors.

From what has been said, it can be seen that the parent company boards for Royal Dutch Petroleum and Shell Transport and Trading have nineteen members, but only three 'executive directors', namely Jeroen van der Veer and Rob Routs (Royal Dutch) and Malcolm Brinded (Shell).

SHELL'S OIL AND GAS RESERVES

In January 2004 the Shell group announced that it was downgrading its reserves by 20 per cent. The question of accounting for oil and gas reserves – 'booking' reserves – is important because it provides a signal to the stock market and investors of the amount of reserves available for the group to exploit in the future. So the public announcement of a downgrade of 20 per cent of its reserves was a serious matter and the share price of Shell Transport and Trading reacted quickly with an 8 per cent fall (see Figure 6). Market concern at the announcement even led to a fall in the share price of Shell's UK rival, BP.[6] It later transpired that there had been questions raised at a fairly high level internally about the state of the reserves in early 2002. In an internal report published in April 2004 by Shell[7] it became evident that the head of exploration and production, Walter van de Vijver, had concerns about the level of reserves being overstated in February 2002 and had forwarded a note to the Committee of Managing Directors, warning that 2.3bn barrels of oil equivalent could be non-compliant with Securities and Exchange Commission (SEC) rules. In other words, the amount booked for reserves was over-optimistic in relation to the rules operated by the US SEC.

But there are also problems with the way the SEC defines reserves. It has been argued that the SEC's definitions were drawn up at a time when modern seismic technology did not exist. Bruce Evers, an analyst at Investec, was quoted as saying that:

> SEC regulations on the way in which you measure and disclose recoverable reserves of oil are themselves debatable. Shell was stuck between a rock and a hard place. There are vagaries about the measurement and estimation of the reserves process and no one is ever going to agree on those numbers. You can call in 10 different firms of consultants and get 10 different answers probably across quite a wide range. So disclosures might be better within a range or a probability of accuracy rather than simply saying there are 442 barrels of oil out there that are recoverable. (Evans, 2004: 43)

One key statistic in this saga is the reserve replacement ratio or RRR. Because an energy company is constantly using up its reserves in production, it therefore needs to ensure that its reserves are being replaced on a regular basis. This can be achieved by carrying out exploration activities that lead to the discovery of new reserves. For a company to remain in a steady state, it would need to achieve a RRR of 100 per cent. A figure higher than 100 per cent indicates that a company has the ability to expand its production in the future. But a figure lower than 100 per cent means that the company is exploiting its reserves faster than it can replace them and therefore faces the possibility of reduced production in the future, unless of course it can make up the deficit in the near future. Thus the RRR signifies the extent to which an energy company has the ability to replace its reserves. This is an important signal to the market and it eventually became apparent that reserves had been over-booked by Shell for a number of years.

The impact of the reduced reserves disclosure on the market was quite dramatic (see Figure 6). Some analysts were reported to be furious at the announcement.[8] One Merrill Lynch analyst changed his rating on Shell from 'buy' to 'neutral', saying, 'This will be the third consecutive year that Shell's reserve replacement will be lower than 100 per cent, raising questions over the sustainability of future growth'.[9] In addition, the share price of Shell had fallen relative to the FTSE World Oil and Gas Sector, which might indicate that news of the reserves position had leaked to the market before the official announcement on 9 January 2004. Certainly, it appeared that the share price of Shell, in the months leading up to February 2004, had fallen relative to other major oil and gas companies.

The share price movements over the year to June 2004 have some interesting implications for efficient markets theory. A supporter of strong form

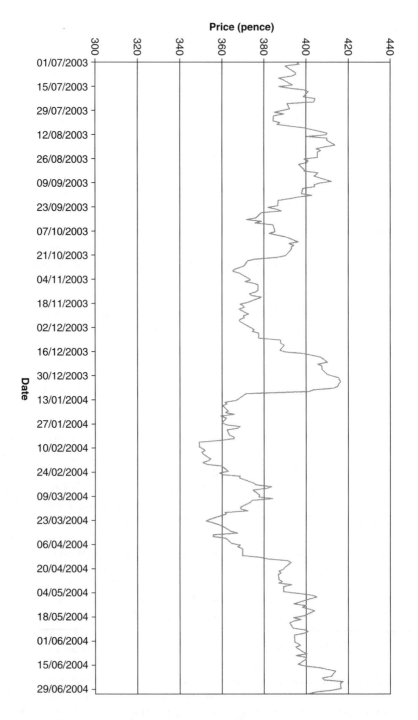

Figure 6 Shell share price, July 2003 to June 2004

Source: Datastream

efficiency might argue that the share price decline, even before the 9 January 2004 announcement, was evidence that the market price could impound information not publicly available. However, there are concerns that such information is essentially insider information and therefore investors who do not have access to this information are placed at a considerable disadvantage to those who do. The substantial drop in share price immediately following the 9 January disclosure might be regarded as evidence of semi-strong form market efficiency. That is, the impact of the reserves information being released to the public caused the share price to fall.

THE INTERNAL INQUIRY

In the internal report prepared by Shell with the help of its lawyers, Davis Polk and Wardwell, it was confirmed that Sir Philip Watts and Walter van de Vijver had been at odds for some time.[10] Walter van de Vijver had succeeded Sir Philip Watts as chief executive of Shell exploration and production in June 2001 and he soon became aware that reserves had been overstated for some time prior to his appointment. But van de Vijver's predicament was that if he tried to criticize the previous procedures for accounting for reserves, he was implicitly criticizing the methods used by his boss, Sir Philip Watts. In a note to the influential Committee of Managing Directors, van de Vijver stated that 2.3bn barrels of oil equivalent were exposed because of non-compliance with SEC rules. However, Sir Philip Watts wanted Shell to achieve a 100 per cent RRR. Clearly the approaches of van de Vijver and Sir Philip Watts were incompatible.

The internal report into the reserves issue referred to deficiencies in controls and the fact that the internal reserves audit was carried out by an 'understaffed and undertrained' ex-employee. 'The booking of 'aggressive' reserves and their continued place on Shell's books were only possible because of certain deficiencies in controls'.[11] In December 2003, the exploration and production staff drafted a memo stating that 2.3bn barrels of oil equivalent of proved reserves were non-compliant but van de Vijver wanted the memo destroyed. But on 9 January 2004, Shell finally admitted to the overstated reserves and on 3 March 2004 Sir Philip Watts and Walter van de Vijver resigned.

Although in 2002 Shell had wanted to report a RRR of 100 per cent, by May 2004 when the annual report and accounts were published it could only claim that its RRR in 2003 was 63 per cent. This contrasts for example with an RRR for Exxon Mobil over 100 per cent for 2001 to 2003, and that for BP over 150 per cent for 2001–2003.[12]

The internal report also stated that outside directors and the group audit committee did not receive the information that would have given them an opportunity to identify or address the issue. Lord Oxburgh, who was non-executive chairman of Shell Transport and Trading, is quoted as saying 'The committee had tried to get hold of the information for a long time but had failed'.[13] John Hofmeister, who was director of human resources at Shell, was quoted as saying that the issue of restating reserves could have been raised through audit, human resources or the non-executive process. In other words Walter van de Vijver could have raised the issue within the company. But this was denied by Walter van de Vijver, who said that he was not in a position to bypass his boss, Sir Philip Watts: 'Because the unspoken rule within the company is that you are not supposed to go directly to individual board members or the group audit committee, I had to rely on the chairman and chief financial officer to advise the group audit committee and assumed that happened in early December [2003]'.[14]

The reserves downgrading made on 9 January 2004 was not the end of the matter and there were several (though smaller) downgrades later that year. By July 2004 Shell had made four separate downgrades of its reserves amounting to 23 per cent of total reserves or 4.47bn barrels of oil equivalent. Soon investors were becoming concerned and on 18 June 2004 it was reported that the group would set up a committee to review its governance procedures and in particular it intended to simplify its complex dual-board structure.[15]

On 25 June 2004 it was reported that two large shareholders in Royal Dutch/Shell called for the company to include investor representatives on the committee that would review its governance and structure. The two shareholders making this request were Knight Vinke, a US asset manager, and Calpers (California Public Employees' Retirement System) and it appears that these large investors were able to exert some influence over the way the review would be carried out. Some idea of the enormous size of Calpers can be judged from the fact that at one time its annual growth was said to be more than sufficient to buy the entire common stock of General Motors.[16] Investors' sentiments also were not helped by news that Sir Philip Watts, the former chairman, would receive a payout of £1m in addition to an annual pension of £584,000.

SHELL FACES ITS CRITICS

In the Shell Transport and Trading Annual Report and Accounts for 2003, Malcolm Brinded, Managing Director and Vice-Chairman of the Committee of Managing Directors stated:

> All shareholders will know of the exceptional circumstances that have delayed the publication of this report. The Group's performance in 2003 will clearly be seen in the context of the restatement of reserves (a reduction of 4.47bn barrels or some 23 per cent from the previously reported end-2002 figures), and the subsequent related management changes of early 2004. These events have understandably caused considerable concern to shareholders, and I know that we have much to do to restore your confidence.

It is vital to ensure that these problems cannot happen again. That is why the Group Audit committee commissioned a rigorous external review of the events and background to these issues and we are implementing its recommendations. They include ensuring strict compliance with the rules and guidance of the Securities and Exchange Commission; a range of measures to strengthen our business controls; ensuring that the Committee of Managing Directors and the Group Audit Committee take a formal role in reviewing the booking of reserves; and the systematic use of external reserves expertise to provide challenge and assurance at critical points in the reserves booking and reporting process. (Shell Transport and Trading, *Annual Report and Accounts 2003*: 3)

On 28 June 2004, annual general meetings were held in the Netherlands and in Britain. At the London annual general meeting on 28 June 2004, Lord Oxburgh as chairman of Shell Transport and Trading offered sincere apologies to UK-based shareholders and Malcolm Brinded, head of exploration and production, offered sincere regrets. One investor was quoted as saying at the annual general meeting 'When somebody is asked to leave under a shadow and yet paid a huge amount of money, it is usually to keep them quiet, isn't it?' and another investor asked why directors had received pay increases of 20 and 30 per cent when the dividend had increased by only 3 per cent.[17]

It emerged at the annual general meeting in the Netherlands that the most senior non-executive director of Royal Dutch Petroleum, Aad Jacobs, had been aware of the reserves problem two months before the public disclosure was made on 9 January 2004. It was reported that Aad Jacobs became aware of an imminent problem with reserves in November 2003 when he had lunch with Walter van de Vijver. This contrasts with comments from Lord Oxburgh, the most senior non-executive director of the UK arm, Shell Transport and Trading. He had denied accusations of a 'cover-up', blaming former executives for being 'economical with the truth' and stating that 'It's very difficult to see how the reserves issue could have come to light sooner'.[18]

In July 2004 the International Energy Agency (IEA) announced that it wanted to see some movement towards a mandatory global standard for accounting for oil and gas reserves, on the ground that there are no consistent rules on oil reserves.[19] No doubt this announcement was partly due to the question of oil and gas reserves at Shell. However, the IEA view conflicted with that of the Securities and Exchange Commission (SEC), which seemed to be in favour of greater disclosure but on a voluntary basis. It could be argued that the subjectivity of the rules for accounting for oil and gas reserves appears to be one of the reasons why oil companies can arrive at different valuation bases.

July 2004 also saw reports that Shell was moving towards a more radical reform of its organizational and corporate governance structures. By this time, Sir John Kerr had been named as the non-executive director of Shell Transport and Trading who would chair the review. Among the changes being considered by the review team were the creation of a unified board with an independent chairman and a single chief executive.

Shell's troubles were set to continue. Standard and Poor's, the international credit ratings agency, expressed concern about the scope of the reforms to be implemented by Shell. Standard and Poor's had previously decided to report on the corporate governance of individual companies, given the scale of corporate failures since the late 1990s. The report described the group's corporate governance profile as moderate to weak, on a five-point scale ranging from very strong and strong, through moderate, to weak and very weak. So the report by Standard and Poor's was not very encouraging, although it was positive about moves made by Shell to improve its corporate governance.[20]

On 30 July 2004 it was reported that Shell had paid fines totalling $151m in order to end disputes with the US Securities and Exchange Commission and the UK Financial Services Authority.

> The SEC had accused the Anglo-Dutch group of having breached fraud, internal control and reporting provisions. The FSA said the company had committed market abuse. Shell did not admit or deny the accusations, calling the settlement a 'hopeful step for Shell'. (*Financial Times*, 30 July 2004: 1)

By now, the new head of Shell, Jeroen van der Veer, chairman of the Committee of Managing Directors, was finding much of his time taken up with reviewing systems and procedures, and dealing with investors. It was perhaps inevitable that this would detract from an important part of his job, which was to pursue exploration and increase production. Finding oil would be a key to Shell's recovery and improve its RRR. It would also make it less likely that Shell would find itself a target by another major oil company.

DISCUSSION

The year 2004 turned out to be tumultuous for Shell. Once the public announcement of reduction in reserves had been made on 9 January 2004 there was a tendency by the company to blame human failings by its top executives rather than criticize structural weaknesses. The company revealed that e-mails between Sir Philip Watts and Walter van der Vijver showed that the two were well aware of the reserves problem some time before the public announcement of 9 January 2004 (Hanney, 2004: 45).

Over the succeeding months, and under pressure from large institutional investors, the company began to institute reviews and appeared to recognize that it has an unusually complicated organization, though it claims that this structure has served the group well for nearly one hundred years and is partly justified by the differing tax and legal regimes in the UK and the Netherlands. Nevertheless, judging by reports in early 2004, the group seems to be moving towards a more unified board structure with an independent chairman and a single chief executive.

An editorial in the *Financial Times* in July 2004 succinctly summed up the problems facing Shell and, in a wider context, the problems facing the international oil and gas industry. The editorial argued that there were two lessons for the oil industry to be learned from the Shell experience:

> One is the need for stricter adherence to guidelines about reserves. The area of ambiguity is not really whether oil and gas deposits exist under-ground; no one has suggested that Shell just dreamed up its oil and gas, and even if it did, a geological deposit can be checked like a bank deposit. The issue is the degree to which deposits are considered marketable enough for an oil company to book them on its balance sheet. This is a matter of judgement . . . The other lesson is the importance of high standards of corporate behaviour in an industry that operates in some of the most corrupt and poorest parts of the world. Oil companies are already very suspect to many local populations and non-governmental organisations who might well wonder, with Shell in mind, whether a management that lied to its biggest shareholders would have any compunction doing the same to Nigerian villagers. Oil companies cannot escape a responsibility to improve standards where they operate. But Shell has made it harder for them to lead by example. (*Financial Times*, 30 July 2004)

One of the problems facing Shell in 2002/3 was that, even though it was recognized by some senior executives that reserves had been overstated, it was not clear how the overstatement should be managed. There are two ways in which reserves can be 'increased'. One method is to look again at existing reserves and argue that they are now more marketable than was previously realized. Another method is for the oil company to physically carry out new exploration activity and find additional reserves. In terms of improving the RRR, the former method is obviously cheaper and quicker than the second method, which could take years and would involve considerable expenditure. This may explain why Sir Philip Watts seemed keen to revise the existing reserves, even sending an e-mail to Walter van de Vijver stating that he should leave no stone unturned to get a 100 per cent replacement ratio.[21]

In August 2004 it was announced by Shell that the former head of exploration and production, Walter van de Vijver, would receive €3.8m (£2.6m) in severance pay. Influential investors did not appear to be unduly perturbed by the size of the severance payment, instead focusing on the plans by the group to reform corporate governance procedures. It was also reported that the former chairman, Sir Philip Watts, had received a severance payment of £1m but neither had received performance bonuses in 2003 or 2004. The payment to Walter van de Vijver was reported to be subject to continued co-operation with authorities investigating the scandal surrounding the booking of oil reserves.[22]

In August 2004 it was also reported that Royal Dutch/Shell faced a possible takeover. The report said that insiders at Royal Dutch/Shell were concerned that Total SA, Europe's no. 3 oil company, was considering making a takeover bid.[23] Although the possibility of Shell being taken over was not high, the fact that such stories could be related with some credibility was perhaps a measure of the seriousness of the problems Shell was facing. And in October 2004, Shell began a substantial asset disposal programme (estimated at $10 billion to $12 billion) in which it would sell underperforming and non-core operations in order to improve its exploration and production activities.

In less than a year, the group had experienced a substantial turnaround in its fortunes. In January 2004 Shell had appeared not too concerned when it cut its estimate of proven reserves and it was reported that Shell was adamant that the cut in reserves would not materially change the volume of oil and gas that the company expected to recover.[24] But in less than two months, two key executives had resigned over the issue and by July 2004 Shell was making moves to radically reform its organizational and corporate governance structures.

Table 12.1 Shell: key events

1897	Shell Transport and Trading created
1907	Formation of Royal Dutch/Shell Group of companies
February 2002	Head of exploration and production expresses concern about overstatement of reserves
January 2004	Shell announces 20% downgrade in its reserves; share price falls by 8%
March 2004	Sir Philip Watts (chairman) and Walter van de Vijver (head of exploration and production) resign
June 2004	Shell announces a review of its corporate governance procedures
July 2004	US Securities and Exchange Commission fines Shell $151 million

Discussion questions

1 To what extent were the events facing Shell in 2004 caused by human failings or structural (organizational) failings?
2 Discuss the potential difficulties facing the members of the parent companies in attempting to monitor and control the activities of management.
3 Is it desirable that oil companies should be allowed to exercise discretion over how they book oil and reserves?
4 Since the market will sooner or later determine if reserves have been overstated, does it matter that overbooking can take place?

5 Why might the senior management of a large quoted company be sensitive to the concerns of large institutional investors such as Calpers?

6 Which stakeholders were most affected by the events at Shell in 2004?

REFERENCES

Evans, C. (2004) 'Shell-shocked', *Accountancy*, May: 42–3.

Hanney, B. (2004) 'Hanged by email: lessons from Shell', *Accountancy*, June: 45–6.

Mallin, C.A. (2004) *Corporate Governance*. Oxford: Oxford University Press.

NOTES

1 For the sake of clarity the name 'Shell' will generally be used in this chapter to refer to the whole group.

2 Source: Shell web site: www.shell.com.

3 Source: Royal Dutch Petroleum Company, *Annual Report and Accounts 2003*.

4 Source: www.corporatewatch.org.uk.

5 Details of boards' membership from Royal Dutch Petroleum Company, *Annual Report and Accounts 2003*. See Mallin, 2004: 125 for a comparison of differences between board structures in European countries.

6 *Independent*, 10 January 2004, Business: 21.

7 *Financial Times*, 20 April 2004: 25.

8 *Observer*, 11 January 2004, Business: 1.

9 *Independent*, 10 January 2004, Business: 21.

10 *Financial Times*, 20 April 2004: 25.

11 *Financial Times*, 20 April 2004: 25.

12 *Financial Times*, 24 April 2004: M3.

13 *Financial Times*, 20 April 2004: 25.

14 *Financial Times*, 29 April 2004: 21.

15 *Financial Times*, 18 June 2004: 1.

16 See R.A.G. Monks and N. Minnow, *Corporate Governance*, 3rd edn, 2004: 135.

17 *Financial Times*, 29 June 2004: 24.

18 *Financial Times*, 29 June 2004: 1.

19 *Financial Times*, 5 July 2004.

20 *Financial Times*, 23 July 2004: 22.

21 Hanney, 2004: 45.

22 *Financial Times*, 13 August 2004: 21.

23 *Observer*, 15 August 2004, Business: 1.

24 *Independent*, 10 January 2004, Business: 21.

Conclusion

The importance of corporate governance lies in the fact that it attempts to deal with conflicts of interest between the interested parties in an organization. A main purpose of this book has been to introduce the reader to a variety of actual cases in business life where corporate governance is seen to be an issue, and to shed light on some of the connections between those events and corporate governance theory and regulation. Although the focus has been on past events, it is reasonable to argue that examining the past is important because it can provide clues as to how corporate governance procedures should be modified in the future.

Not all the cases have reached a decisive outcome, however. It is in the nature of these events that it can be many years before 'closure' occurs. For instance, in 2004, legal actions were continuing in respect of Enron and WorldCom. Parmalat was being restructured while Shell addressed its organizational and corporate governance structures. Polly Peck legal proceedings are unlikely to resume until Asil Nadir returns to the UK. The liquidators of BCCI are suing the Bank of England in a legal case that could continue until 2006.

The reader may well feel at this point that some particular issues seem to have a habit of recurring in different cases. This chapter aims, therefore, to review some common themes that tend to run through the actual examples in the book. One issue that most would agree on is that in each case there was a conflict between the interests of the managers and other stakeholders.

THREE SPECIAL CASES

First, it may be useful to separate three cases from the rest. These are Eurotunnel, Barings and Shell. Eurotunnel represents a special case of a breakdown in trust between the board of directors and the shareholders. This was evidenced in April 2004 when the shareholders, at the annual general meeting, sacked the chairman and chief executive. The curious point about Eurotunnel was that the anger of the shareholders seems to have been directed at a board of directors as it existed in 2004. But those directors had not been present at the time of the initial share floatation and construction, the period to which Eurotunnel's problems could be traced. Those directors had retired or resigned by 2004. In fact it could be argued that the Eurotunnel management in place at the beginning of 2004 was acting quite effectively, in terms of the financial and commercial strategies it was pursuing. Were the interests of the shareholders best served by the vote that ousted the chairman and chief executive on 7 April 2004? A definitive answer may not be forthcoming for some time. But when the chairman and chief executive were sacked, the share price stood at 38p. Four months later, at the beginning of August 2004, the share price had fallen to 14p.

Barings represents an unusual case of a bank which failed primarily through the activities of one of its derivatives traders, Nick Leeson. Paradoxically, trading in derivatives, such as options and futures contracts, is often seen as a way of reducing risk if used properly. It is true that fraud took place when Leeson forged documents in an attempt to support his claim that Barings were owed £50m from a broking firm, but there is no evidence that there was collusion at the level of the board of directors. The evidence appears to indicate that Leeson resorted to fraud in order to disguise the losses he had made, and not to enrich himself. The senior management of Barings were not aware of the extent to which trading in derivatives could massively increase risk.

Shell is an interesting example of a company that faced problems when it was forced to publicly acknowledge that its oil and gas reserves had been overstated. The news became public in January 2004 and the consequences for Shell included a large and immediate fall in its share price, the resignation of senior staff and fines paid to the Securities and Exchange Commission (SEC) and Financial Services Authority (FSA). In addition, Shell has had to carry out a review of its organizational structures and corporate governance procedures.

COLLAPSES WITH SOME COMMON CAUSES

The remaining cases concern Maxwell, Polly Peck, BCCI, Enron, WorldCom and Parmalat. A number of common themes run through some of these cases.

Too much power in the hands of the chairmen and chief executives

Concern is often expressed if too much power resides in the hands of the chairman and chief executive of an organization. In particular, if one person holds both posts, it would take a strong independent element on the board to challenge that person's authority. It is often the case that, by their nature, the people who lead large organizations have had to take difficult business decisions in their progress to the top and they are often charismatic and powerful figures in their own right. The Cadbury Report (1992) expressed concern about the potential dangers of concentrating too much power in the hands of one or two top executives and *The Combined Code on Corporate Governance* (2003) recommends that there should be a clear division of responsibilities at the head of the company between running the board and the executive responsibility for running the company's business. In the UK, separation of the posts of chairman and chief executive is seen as advisable. But it is curious that in the United States this characteristic is seen as less problematic.

Spectacular share price performance

In some cases, the share price performed beyond reasonable expectations, sometimes over long periods. This applied to Polly Peck, Enron and WorldCom. Any shareholders who were fortunate enough to invest over a long period, and sell out months before the final collapse, were able to realize substantial capital gains. On the other hand, those left holding shares at the date of the collapse lost virtually their entire investments.

Share support operations

There is some evidence that Maxwell and Polly Peck made strenuous efforts to maintain their share price in the months before collapse. Maxwell pledged shares to support the share price of Maxwell Communications Corporation and Mirror Group Newspapers. When shares were used as collateral for loans, the danger was that a falling share price would prompt the lender to seek additional security.

Complexity of financial statements and structures

Financial statement complexity applied to Maxwell, BCCI, Enron and Parmalat. Enron used particularly complicated forms of off-balance sheet financing in order to disguise the true level of debt in the organization. Maxwell, BCCI and Parmalat used a variety of companies in different countries and under different jurisdictions in order to disguise the flow of funds. This made it exceptionally difficult to disentangle and interpret the true state of the groups' affairs.

Audit function

The audit function is often criticized after the event and this applied particularly to Enron and WorldCom. The audit firm for both companies was Arthur Andersen which (as a result of these company failures) itself no longer exists. In fact, the US Sarbanes–Oxley Act of 2002 specifically refers to the need to separate audit and non-audit services. The UK *Combined Code on Corporate Governance* is less forceful, simply requiring the annual report to state how independence is safeguarded if the auditor provides non-audit services.

Board of directors

The UK *Combined Code on Corporate Governance* emphasizes the importance of independent non-executive directors in maintaining public confidence in the conduct of the company. US regulations also stress the importance of independent directors, although this is largely achieved through stock exchange listing requirements. As regards Maxwell, Polly Peck, Enron and WorldCom, the boards of directors were criticized for not exercising a sufficiently strong influence on the main actors.

Legal action against analysts and journalists

The Maxwell case shows how financial analysts and journalists had to cope with the threat of legal action if they considered criticizing Maxwell's companies. Parmalat at one point asked Consob, the Italian regulator, to investigate financial institutions which had expressed reservations about the company's finances.

Relationship with banks and financial institutions

Maxwell, WorldCom and Parmalat are examples where some banks and financial institutions failed to maintain a sufficiently objective relationship with their client company. In the case of WorldCom, Citigroup announced in May 2004 that it would pay $2.65 billion to settle investor lawsuits resulting from WorldCom's financial problems.

Whistleblowers

In the case of Enron, Sherron Watkins made considerable efforts to bring her concerns to the attention of her superiors. At WorldCom, Cynthia

Cooper was instrumental in bringing dubious accounting transactions to the attention of the audit committee. It is interesting that the Sarbanes–Oxley Act now contains specific provisions to protect employees who raise concerns about potential criminal offences.

Fraud

Fraud occurs in several cases. Fraud and deception appear to have taken place over a long period at Parmalat. Fraud was also a central issue over a number of years in the case of BCCI. In 2004, senior Enron directors were facing fraud charges. It might be useful to distinguish between cases where the perpetrators committed fraud in order to unduly enrich themselves, and cases where fraud was used as perhaps a final and desperate attempt to delay bankruptcy proceedings.

Creative accounting

Creative accounting features in several cases. In the case of Enron, some of the off-balance sheet financing schemes were very sophisticated and clearly designed to give a favourable impression of the company's debt position. In the case of WorldCom, creative accounting was used to disguise operating expenses as capitalized expenditures in order to reduce depreciation charges in the profit-and-loss account (and therefore show higher reported profits). In the case of Parmalat, the reporting of non-existent cash deposits went far beyond what could be termed 'creative accounting' and was clearly fraudulent.

Finally, as was stated in Chapter 1, this book does not pretend to offer easy solutions to the issues raised in the case studies. Each case is unique and hopefully provides a fascinating insight into human behaviour. It is unlikely that complete consensus will ever be achieved over what is 'good' corporate governance. However, this book will have served a useful purpose if it has helped to promote discussion of the main issues identified in the case studies.

REFERENCES

Cadbury Report (1992) *Report of the Committee on the Financial Aspects of Corporate Governance*. London: Gee Publishing.

Financial Reporting Council (2003) *The Combined Code on Corporate Governance*. London: Financial Reporting Council.

Sarbanes–Oxley Act of 2002. *Public Law 107–204*. Washington, DC, 30 July.

Index

Added to a page number 'f' denotes a figure, 't' denotes a table and 'n' denotes notes.